ETTORE MAIOTTI
The Drawing Handbook

Learning from the Masters

Clarkson N. Potter, Inc./Publishers
New York

Those drawings not otherwise cited are
those of Ettore Maiotti

English translation copyright © 1989 by Gruppo
Editoriale Fabbri, S.p.A.

Copyright © 1989 by Gruppo Editoriale Fabbri, S.p.A.

Copyright © 1989 by Cosmopress, Geneva, for the works
of Paul Klee

Translated by Kerry Milis Parker

Published in 1989 by Clarkson N. Potter, Inc.,
201 East 50 St., New York, New York 10022.

CLARKSON N. POTTER, POTTER, and
colophon are trademarks of Clarkson N. Potter, Inc.

Manufactured in Italy
by Gruppo Editoriale Fabbri S.p.A., Milan

Library of Congress Cataloging-in-Publication Data

Maiotti, Ettore
The Drawing Handbook: learning from the masters/
Ettore Maiotti.
p.   cc.

ISBN 0-517-57283-4: $ 12.95
1. Drawing--Technique. I. Title.
NC730. M245 1989   88-26902
741.2--dc 19   CIP

ISBN 0-517-57283-4
10 9 8 7 6 5 4 3 2 1

First American Edition

CONTENTS

INTRODUCTION

I remember my first "real" drawing very well. It was a portrait of a classmate I drew during a mathematics test in my second year at a trade school.

Before the school system changed over to one of comprehensive schools, students who were not planning to go to college attended schools that trained them for some kind of trade. By the time you were fourteen, formal education was at an end and you went out into the world of work.

My teacher had advised my parents to encourage me to attend such a school because I had shown so little interest in academic subjects and was very lax in my study habits. I certainly made very little progress in the courses that were prescribed for us: in the morning, we had general basic studies and in the afternoon we learned carpentry and mechanics.

And so it was during a math test that I tried for the first time to draw from life a portrait of my classmate. Let me briefly try to explain how this happened. Normally during an exam, I would desperately try to copy from my neighbors, paying no attention whatsoever to what I wrote down. I was not even very careful about choosing someone from whom to crib, and I usually ended up copying right and wrong answers alike. One morning while I was waiting for my neighbor to work out some solutions, I became distracted and began to look at his profile with great interest. I started to sketch it on my test paper. Wanting to get it right, I got so involved in my drawing, that I worked with great intensity just as I do now, and for the first time in my life, I felt happy, even pleased with myself.

Such ardor, so unlike my normal attitude, must have awakened the curiosity of my teacher, for he came over and stood quietly behind me. He let me finish my drawing and then he kindly asked me if he could keep it. Of course, I did not do very well on my math test, but the teacher encouraged me to follow my interest and to find my vocation in the world of art.

Many years went by before I decided to pursue my interests in any dedicated or disciplined way. I wasted a lot of time drawing mediocre caricatures before I finally summoned up the courage to throw myself heart and soul into drawing. Then I began to draw everything with great zeal. Drawing was my first love, and I tried to express everything in that medium, before moving on to color and before growing to love painting.

Today, after years of working as an artist, I still draw all the time and with as much enthusiasm; in fact, every one of my abstract paintings is preceded by a figurative drawing. And when I draw, I still become so absorbed in my task that I completely forget everything around me, including the time.

I think drawing offers enormous possibilities for expressing the human soul. If you study the drawings of the old masters beginning with the Renaissance, (particularly those of Leonardo da Vinci), and work your way to the present, you will discover something wonderful: the drawings are alive and have the power to influence and move us. And once you are able not only to copy such drawings, but also to see and to interpret the reality of the great masters for yourself, you will start to look at the world of painting more critically and realistically. With this book, I hope to introduce you to the artist's universe and teach you to look at the world from a different perspective so that you will come to understand and love it in a whole new way. I also hope to pass on to you a passion for drawing. If you encourage this passion, it will repay the energy you devote to it many times over.

Ettore Maiotti

THE PENCIL

A Short History

Before the discovery of graphite in Cumberland, England, in the second half of the sixteenth century, artists drew with styluses made of an alloy of tin and lead or silver, or of brass. The stylus were used mostly to draw on paper. Sticks of charcoal or hematite (sanguine or drawing charcoal) were also used.

With the invention of the pencil these styluses were gradually abandoned; today they are found only in specialized stores.

The Making of a Pencil

There are two basic types of pencil sold commercially. One is a strip of graphite encased in a wooden cylinder and the other is the mechanical pencil.

Graphite passes through several stages before it ends up in a pencil. First it must be crushed, a process that takes from 150 hours for an inexpensive pencil to 600 hours for one of the highest quality.

Large tanks are filled one-third full with porcelain balls nearly a foot in diameter. Graphite and clay are poured into the tanks in proportions that determine the ultimate hardness of the lead. The hardness of graphite is measured on a scale of nineteen degrees. Water is added and the tank is rotated, causing the balls to roll and break down the pieces of graphite into tiny, crystalline flakes. When this operation is over, the water is drained away through a filter press, and the remaining mixture is blended with enough water to make a thick homogeneous paste. This paste then passes through a loading funnel onto a conveyor belt, and into a compression chamber, which forces air out of the mixture and makes it even smoother. From there, it enters a tube that cuts the mixture into very fine strands.

These newly formed strands are reshaped in a vacuum press into what looks like loaves of bread — cylinders about sixteen inches long and four inches in diameter. Again, the loaves are cut into fine strands, each at least seven inches long. They are places in a perforated basket and passed through a drying oven, where they are rotated as they move along.

After cooling for three hours, the strands are returned to a sealed, fire-proof container and baked again at 1832-2012 F. Double baking is necessary for leads; colored pastels do not need a second baking, because the clay of the graphite blend has not yet hardened enough to serve its function as binder and stabilizer.

After the leads cool, they are passed through a wax bath and are finally ready to be inserted in wooden cases. The graphite leads are selected for encasing and placed on an assembly line.

The wooden cylinders for pencil casings are made from California cedar. Long rods of a standard diameter are cut and a groove cut along the length of each rod. Glue is spread along this groove and the leads are placed in the cavity. Finally, a second grooved piece of wood is fitted over the embedded lead to form a kind of sandwich.

After these "sandwiches" have passed through inspection, they are placed in a pressurized oven and subjected to a temperature of 302 degrees Fahrenheit.

When they have finished baking and have cooled down, they are at last cut into pencil lengths. All they need now is to be varnished, stamped with their brand name and degree of hardness, and sharpened to a point.

Graphite is available not only encased in a pencil, but also as a square stick, without the wooden case.

Stages in the manufacture of drawing pencils, from the mixing of graphite with clay to the encasing of the graphite in the wood pencils and finishing operations.

8

Pencil with Different Degrees of Hardness

Series B pencils have soft leads while series H have hard ones. Here is a scale showing how dark a tone each pencil can make, reflecting its degree of hardness:

Very soft leads used for dark shading (8B, 7B, 6B, 5B)

Soft leads used for sketching and architectural drawings (4B, 3B, 2B)

Soft leads used for drawing, writing and stenography (B, HB, F)

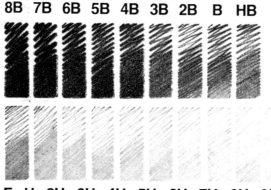

8B 7B 6B 5B 4B 3B 2B B HB

F H 2H 3H 4H 5H 6H 7H 8H 9H

Hard and very hard leads used for technical drawing (H, 2H, 3H, 4H)

Extra-hard, very resistant leads suitable for cartography, lithography and wood-engraving (5H, 6H, 7H, 8H, 9H)

You can see how important it is to know the characteristics of different leads and their technical possibilities so that they can be fully exploited. When you are familiar with their characteristics you will be able to choose the right pencil for any task. Certainly the wrong pencil will adversely affect the results of your work.

With leads of different degrees of hardness you can do many different kinds of drawing. The artist is well aware of the possibilities offered by the vast range of leads. Most drawings will require the use of at least two or three pencils of different hardnesses. For example, for a still life, you might sketch the outlines with a 3B pencil, then construct the shadows with a 2B and finish

How to Sharpen a Pencil

The first thing that you must learn to do to perfection is to sharpen your pencil.

Do not underestimate the importance of sharpening a pencil correctly, as do so many art school students who have never been properly taught. Remember that good draftspersons with high professional standards can be recognized by the sharpness of the points of their pencils.

Naturally, you can use a high-quality pencil sharpener, but a good draftsperson prefers to use

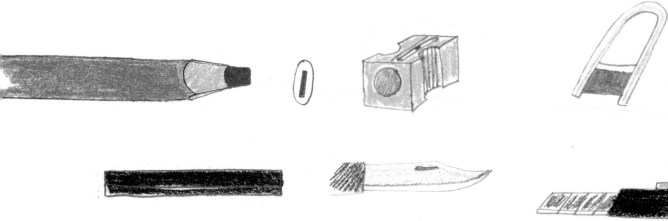

the drawing with a 1B. For outlining the contours of a drawing, painting or sketch, the softest pencil is the most suitable.

a small blade to obtain a laserlike point. Practice on small pieces of wood the size of a pencil, using a sharp knife. Here is how to do it:

First, cut down one side

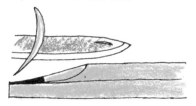

Then, down the opposite side

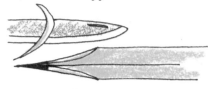

Then, down the other sides

Continue to turn your pencil, sharpening the planes as you go so that eventually you have six sides.

By the time you have filled a shoe box with wood shavings from your efforts, you will have acquired enough experience to carry out this operation properly.

How to Sharpen a Mechanical Pencil
Buy some very fine sandpaper (00 is best), cut it in wide strips, 1 x 4 inches, then find a piece of corrugated cardboard or a piece of cardboard from a shoe box if it is stiff enough and cut out a piece measuring 3 x 4 1/2 inches.
Place four or five strips of sandpaper on the cardboard with the rough side up and staple the ends to the cardboard (see fig. 1).
The extra cardboard extending beyond the sandpaper on each side will allow you to hold the cardboard with one hand while you hold the pencil in the other.
To get a good point, release the lead in the mechanical pencil so it extends about one inch; place the cardboard at the edge of a table, keep-

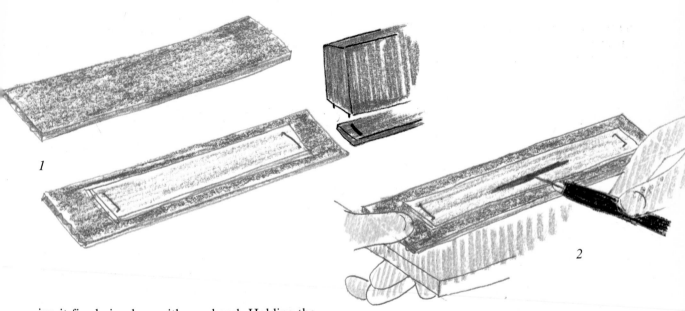

1

2

ing it firmly in place with one hand. Holding the pencil at a 10 degree angle from the sand paper (fig. 2), rub the lead back and forth against it.

Rotate the pencil as you rub, until you have a fine, even point (fig. 3).
Be careful not to push too hard. It is the sandpaper which will sharpen your pencil, not the force of your hand. Otherwise you are in danger of breaking your point.

3

Drawing Surfaces

With a pencil you can draw on just about any surface on which you can write (wood, canvas, a wall); though, of course, paper is the ideal.

Smooth paper is most suitable for technical and architectural drawings or single-line drawings done with hard leads from the H series. Paper with a rough or semirough surface is better for artists' drawings made with the softer B series pencils.

Artists, however, like to experiment with a wide variety of paper, from notepaper to brown wrapping paper (which happens to be what I like best, as well as Canson and tracing paper. You will have your own favorite.

According to many painters, the abovementioned papers give better results if placed on a piece of cardboard for support.

Fixatives

Pencil drawings, no matter what the degree of hardness of the pencil used, need to be preserved with a special liquid that will keep the lines from smudging when they are handled; this way they will last longer.

To preserve your drawing from damage, you must follow a precise method.

Since aerosol sprays are a threat to the environment, it is better to use a bottled fixative and a pump sprayer. The kind of sprayer used to mist flowers works well.

You can make your own fixative if you like. Buy some damar resin and denatured alcohol (90 per cent). Mix one part resin with two parts alcohol and let this mixture sit for several days. Then mist your drawing, holding the sprayer at least sixteen inches from the surface.

For another kind of fixative, mix two parts white lacquer varnish with twenty parts alcohol and put this in a clear bottle, filling it only half full. Let this mixture sit for at least four days, shaking it from time to time.

If you run out of fixative, you can also use a mixture made from a half cup of milk diluted with a half cup of water and one cup of alcohol (which will make it dry faster); shake this solution well, then spray it over your drawing.

I advise you to use a light hand when applying fixatives because the high water content can drench and thus warp the paper.

The Work Position

The position in which you work will vary according to whether you are sketching, working at a table or at an easel.

When you are sketching or working at a table,

there are no precise rules. The important thing is to adopt a comfortable position that will allow you to continue working for several hours. To work at an easel, I advise you to do it the way great painters of the past did, following clearly defined rules that govern the placement of your easel and your subject, and the correct distance between you and the easel.

The great painters of the past followed strict rules as far as painting, as you can read in an extract from *Lives of the Artists* by Giorgio Vasari, who wrote in the sixteenth century:

"In painting, the outline has several uses, of which the first is to indicate the contours of each figure; if it is correctly drawn, with the right proportions, and the right shading and highlights, it will give the figure relief and allow you some very good effects. If you master line you will become proficient through practice and judgment in each of these skills. Similarly, anyone who wants to express in his drawings what his spirit has conceived, or anything else that pleases him, should, after much practice and as a way of perfecting his skills, begin to copy three-dimensional figures: marble or stone statues; plaster-casts taken from nature or from beautiful old objects; clay figures of nudes; and draped cloths, in order to study the folds and draping of the material. All of these immobile, inanimate objects are easy to portray because they do not move about like live models. After one has practiced a great deal and acquired a sure hand when drawing, one can begin to work with live models and achieve through assiduous study an equal mastery in that area. Work that is copied from nature truly brings honor to him who has applied himself diligently; along with a singular grace and liveliness, it has a simplicity, ease and sweetness that can only come from life, something only nature so perfectly reveals. Be assured, and I underline this, that years of practice are the key to drawing and that which creates the best artists".

There are many different kinds of easels available in stores and at many prices, but if you like carpentry, you might like to make your own. Here is how to do it:

You will need three planks of wood measuring six feet by four inches by one inch thick, two boards measuring ten by four by one inch thick, a broomstick, a three-foot long chain, a screw-hook and two hinges.

Apply a coat of a white all-purpose glue, such as Elmer's, to the smaller boards. Nail one of these small boards to two of the planks. These should be positioned so that they form a 30-degree angle to each other. Use long nails that will extend through the board to the other side; pound the part that extends down flat (fig. 1). Stand the two planks on the ground and cut them even with the floor so that they will stand up straight (fig. 2). Cut a length of broomstick to fit between the two planks and screw one end of the broomstick to each plank at a height of one foot above the ground (fig. 3). You will need a drill for this. Now take the second small board and nail the third plank perpendicular to it to form a kind of T. Remember to apply a coat of glue to the surface before you pound in your nails (fig. 4). Now connect the two boards at the top with the hinges, taking care that they are perfectly aligned before you attach them with long screws (fig. 5). Cut the remaining broomstick into two eight-inch lengths to form two cone-shaped pegs (fig. 6). Bore several parallel holes the diameter of the

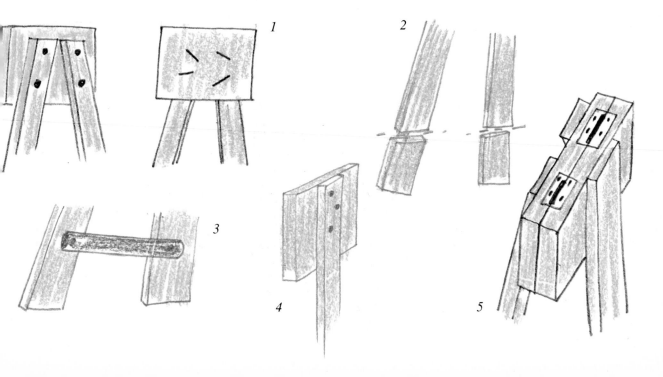

1

2

3

4

5

pegs on each side of the planks (fig. 7). There should be at least five of them on each side about six inches apart. These will allow you to support your canvas at different heights (fig. 8).

Nail one end of the chain to the center of the broomstick handle attached to the two planks. Screw in the screwhook to the other plank at a height of one foot above the ground. This way you can hook the chain at any distance you want (fig. 9). For it to be stable, the legs of the easel, when closed, should be of the same length. While this easel may not be a masterpiece of carpentry, it will be very useful and I guarantee that is easy to make for it is a model of the very first easel I ever made.

Choose as a support a board that extends at least two inches beyond your paper. Do not use plywood or pressed wood for the board, even if it seems very smooth. You will probably want to have several work surfaces in different sizes.

Attach your paper to the board with either thumbtacks or tape. To do this, set your board flat on a table, then tack down the upper corners of your paper to the surface first. Use your hands to smooth down the paper until all the air bubbles have been eliminated, starting with the right-hand side. Now, tack down the lower right-hand corner. Continue smoothing and tacking, finishing with the lower left-hand corner. If the paper is very large, add extra tacks, halfway between the others (fig. 10). Again, the support to which you attach your paper should be of larger size than the paper. To avoid problems, be ready with supports of different sizes. Be careful not to use a pressed wood for your board, because it is not perfectly smooth and will completely spoil your drawing.

Let's go back now to your working position. Use a piece of chalk or crayon to mark the position of the feet of the easel and your own feet on the floor so you can resume the same position if you are interrupted (fig. 11).

Place the axis of the paper so that is directly in front of your arm when you extend it (fig. 12).

12

You should arrange the easel and your subject so that the only things that move are your eyes, and not your whole body (fig. 13).

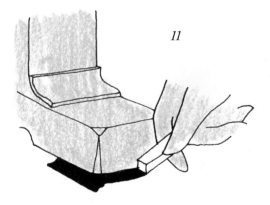

11

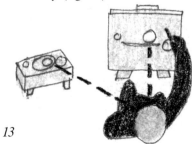

13

14

To find the coordinates of the subject you plan to draw, use a plumb line and a pencil (fig. 14).

A plumb line is a tool used by carpenters and can easily be found in any hardware store. It is a metal weight tied to a string or cord; the weights come in different shapes, some heavier than others. As you are likely to end up holding it for long periods of time, I suggest you buy a lightweight one.

Alternatively, you can make one yourself by attaching any heavy object to a string or by filling a small pouch with pebbles and attaching it to a cord. A curtain pull also works well. The important thing is that the weight of your object pulls the cord down straight and keeps it taut.

How to Use a Plumb Line

Facing your subject, extend your arm in front of you and then drop the plumb line down so it forms a 45 degree angle with your arm. Try to hold it still; do not let it swing.

Now, look at your subject with one eye closed, while you hold the plumb line so that it is between you and what you plan to draw. The plumb line will fall vertically along the length of your subject. By using it as a reference point, you can note on your paper the points of your subject that cross it.

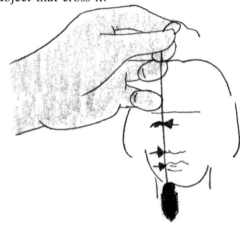

Finding the points along a horizontal line is essentially the same. Hold your pencil horizontally in front of your subject and again, with one eye closed, note the lines that cross it.

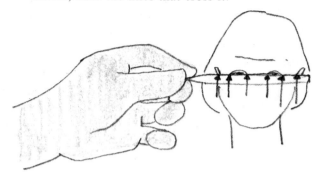

Drawing a Vertical Line

To draw a vertical line, extend your arm in front of you, keeping your back straight. The pencil and your arm should work as a single unit.

Now, rest the point of your pencil on the sheet of paper without letting your fingers touch the paper. Then, as if it were a dead weight, let your arm fall along the paper, without lifting your pencil (fig. 1).

Drawing a Horizontal Line

To draw a horizontal line, take the same position as you did before and move your arm from left to right or right to left (fig. 2).

Maintaining this position as you draw is difficult and requires practice, but do not become dis-

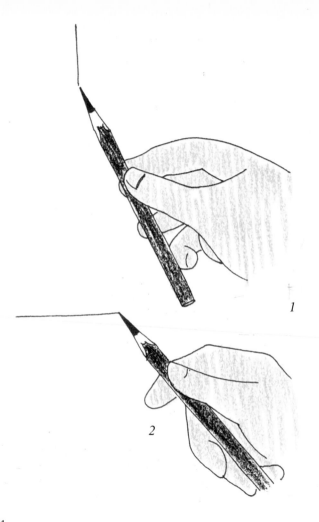

couraged. There is no particular magic involved in learning to draw.

The main thing is to keep on practicing and be diligent about it. I guarantee that this works; I have seen it happen in my classes. For the last year I have been teaching older students who have always wanted to learn to draw but never had the confidence to do so. They have discovered that not only can they draw, but some of them can draw very well.

Do not trust any teacher who tells you you have no talent for drawing — it may be that he or she has no talent for teaching.

Four Easy Exercises

One of the lessons to learn in drawing is symmetry, which you can master with four basic exercises.

The first exercise will familiarize you with the different grades of pencils. Instead of having you fill in meaningless squares with hatching, however, I propose that you try some figures which may prove useful to you later.

For this exercise you will need HB, 1B, 2B and 3B pencils.

You are going to construct a series of lozenges on a sheet of grid paper which you will then turn into a play of lines that form a decorative figure.

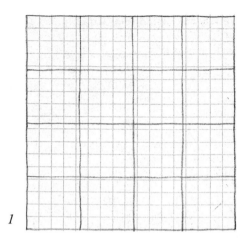

1

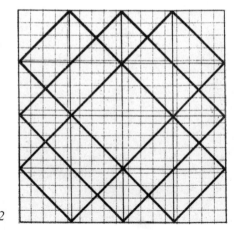

2

To do this, divide your sheet into sixteen squares with an HB pencil (fig. 1). Now hatch each square with diagonal lines using a 2B pencil (fig. 2). Using this as a base, construct a decorative mo-tif, erasing lines as necessary. Now go over the figure again with a 2B pencil, then hatch the large central square with a 3B pencil and the other squares with a 1B (fig. 3).

3

3a

Next crosshatch the triangles along the edge and the inner rectangles, and hatch the inner squares next to them, making them darker (fig. 3a). When you have finished the exercise, spray it with fixative. The project can be repeated using harder pencils on plain unlined paper.

The second exercise I suggest is a study in hatching, symmetry and stylization. With the aid of

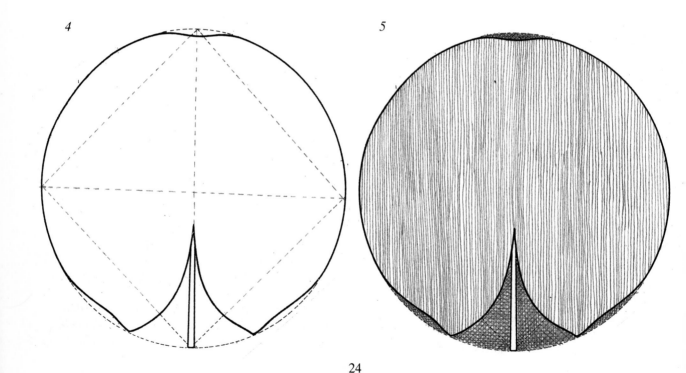

geometric figures, you must turn a circle into a lotus leaf. Do this exercise (figs. 4 and 5) using only series B pencils.

The third exercise to try is reproduced below, half finished. I have left it that way so you can

7

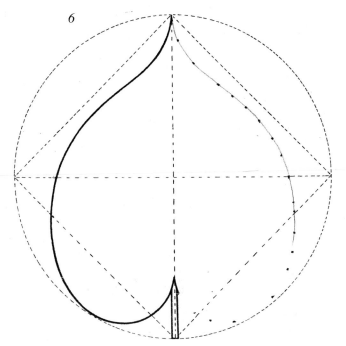

6

8

see how to find the points within the square (fig. 6); finish it by hatching, as you did in the preceding exercise.

The fourth and final exercise consists of taking what you have learned so far and synthesizing it, to create a flower, the wild rose. Compare figure

25

7 with the more detailed drawing of a wild rose in figure 8. It should help you to understand better the way in which the last flower was created. Learning to analyze objects by reducing them to their geometric forms is a basic exercise that accustoms us to reproducing what we see and not what we know. To practice this, gather together many different shaped leaves and flowers, and try to draw their shapes the way we have done the flower described above.

What is a Drawing?

The difference between a Roman mosaic, such as that on page 27 showing Alexander defeating Darius at the battle of Issus in 333 B.C., and a painting by Jean-Auguste-Dominique Ingres (1780-1867) (see p. 28) is not as great as the difference between a painting by Ingres and a work by Paul Klee (1879-1940), even though Ingres and Klee are separated by less than eighty years. At one time, among its other roles, painting served as a visual record, capturing images and preserving them throughout the centuries. With the arrival of new means of visual communication, such as photography, film, television and even computers, figurative and abstract painting began to serve less often as a medium of information and true description than as a type of decoration. This has not been as true of drawing, because drawing represents the creative moment when the artist's thought takes shape. In a drawing, and especially in a sketch, the artist is free to invent new solutions to artistic problems and can eventually integrate them into paintings.

Of course, such innovations have often caused furors and even scandal. Look at the case of Michelangelo who, at twenty-four, portrayed the Virgin Mary in his Pietà, now at Saint Peter's in Rome, with the face of an adolescent girl so young she might have been the younger sister or even the daughter of Christ.

What is wonderful about it, though, beyond theories, is that a sketch, even more than a drawing, is "anarchistic". By this I mean that it is free from all rules — it is creative, constructive, evolving, communicative, poetic....

And this is why, even though more years separate Klee from Michelangelo than from Ingres, if you look at their sketches, it is hard to tell the difference — as you will see from the examples on the following pages.

Alexander's Victory over Darius at Issus, *Roman mosaic from the 2nd century BC, from the House of Faun, Pompei. Museo Archeologico Nazionale, Naples.*

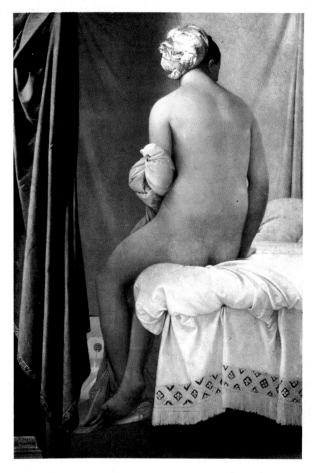

Paul Klee (1879-1940): Senecio, 1922. Oil on canvas (15x16 in.). Kunstmuseum, Basel.

Jean-Auguste-Dominique Ingres (1780-1867): The Valpinçon Bather, 1808. Oil on canvas (55-1/8 x 37-7/16 in.). The Louvre, Paris.

Left: Michelangelo Buonarroti (1475-1564): Caricature of the Artist, *done during work on the vaults of the Sistine Chapel, the Vatican.*

Right: Paul Klee: Nude Dancing with Two Plants, *1907. Soft pencil on paper. Fondation Klee, Berne.*

29

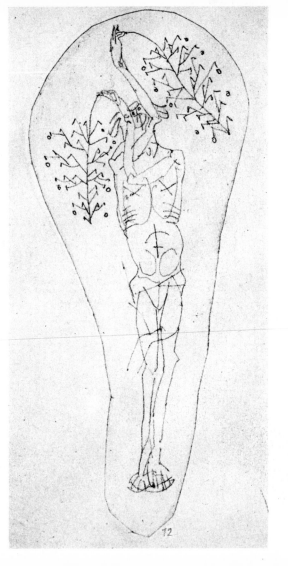

A Plate, Some Knives and a Teapot by van Gogh

I have always admired Vincent van Gogh. In fact, there are times when I almost envy him. Each time I see a reproduction of one of his drawings for the first time, I spend weeks in a frenzy, hoping to get across in my own work some of the same force and intensity he expressed in his.

Van Gogh was able to communicate a powerful force in everything he portrayed. When he first began to draw, he was a very poor draftsman, as were many of the Impressionists, but in the space of ten years (between the ages of twenty-seven and thirty-seven), he succeeded in making his painting into a solid base for all of modern art. Every time I look at one of his drawings I want to shout, "Isn't it beautiful?!"

Once I had a studio in the loft of an old building that was inhabited by a cross-section of humanity absorbed in the most basic problems of survival. Stuck up on one tenant's wall there was a lid from a box of chocolates on which was reproduced van Gogh's painting *Vincent van Gogh's Bedroom*.

These people were certainly not art experts, but they had instinctively chosen that package with that picture and decided to keep it by hanging it

Vincent van Gogh (1853-90): Plate, Knives, and Teapot, 1885. (13-9/16 x 8-1/16 in.). Rijksmuseum, Amsterdam.

30

on the wall. They liked van Gogh even though they knew nothing about him. And I must say that the simple way he expresses things, the way he uses lines, and the way he communicates also pleased me. These are the qualities that I envied in him: Vincent van Gogh made everything he portrayed come alive. I began then to try especially hard to see things as van Gogh saw them, choosing the same objects and working endlessly, copying his methods.

I have reproduced a drawing by van Gogh that I would like you to study carefully.

It was made using a soft pencil. If you look at the plate at the top of the page, you will see that the oval is uneven and the plate seems irregular. An accurate drawing, though, would not have produced the effect of perspective engendered by the shadows along the inner edges. The darkest shadows cast by the plate follow the elliptical movement of the object itself, and give it striking movement and volume.

Look next at the knives and consider the construction of the whole drawing. Van Gogh did not draw two knives and a plate on the table by accident.

He arranged them this way to create an ideal geometric figure. If you look at the drawing you will note that the shadows of the plate and of the knives form a triangle.

31

Now move on to the teapot at the bottom of the page. You will quickly conclude that it must have been added to the composition later. First of all, it does not have the same shadows as the other objects; indeed, it has none.

The energy pouring out of this drawing of simple objects is truly extraordinary, and it is a confirmation of the way Vincent van Gogh succeeded in making inanimate objects, insignificant in themselves, vibrant and alive.

How to Compose a Drawing

I have chosen some simple objects for this exercise, a plate and three onions, items which are easily found in most houses and have very familiar forms.

Begin by analyzing the structure of the onions. They each have an imaginary axis or straight line which divides them into two halves (an ellipsoid). If you look at an onion head-on, you will see that the dried roots can be included in the

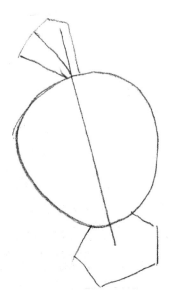

irregular geometric figure.

Once you understand the structure of the onions, you can arrange the composition.

Choose a plain white concave plate and place your three onions in it so that they form the points of a triangle.

When your composition is ready, you can begin to sketch. Keep it small at the beginning: the first few times you draw a composition, your sketch should not be more than about four inches square. Later you might try doing the drawing again, gradually enlarging it, but until you have acquired the necessary ability, it is best to stick to a small format.

Here is how to draw your composition. With a soft 4B pencil, begin by drawing the plate as if the onions were not there; this means drawing the unseen parts as well as those in evidence. Follow this basic rule: divide the plate into quarters, with two imaginary lines intersecting at right angles. You will see that the top left quarter is symmetrical to the bottom right quarter, and the same is true of the other two quarters. This will always hold true, no matter what perspective you choose or what the object is, as long as it is round and viewed as it lies flat. Just imagine you have X-ray vision and use it in your drawings.

Next, sketch the outline of the onions on the plate and fill in the details with a light touch. The drawing should not be too detailed; the impression you achieve is more important than the actual representation.

Notice where any shadows fall and outline these areas in your drawing with the point of your pencil. Now lightly fill them in with hatching, making them darker by simple superimposition.

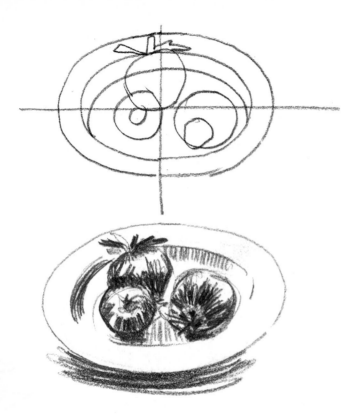

It is very important to avoid starting with dark shading. Remember to start with a very light shading; later you can make it darker by superimposing the shading again and again.

Observing and Drawing Solid Objects

The first important thing to do as you begin to draw is to learn how to read the shapes, shadows, perspectives, and sizes of objects.

Leonardo da Vinci said:

"About the pleasure of painting: The divine character of painting causes the spirit of the painter to be transformed into an image of the spirit of God; he gives himself freely to the creation of diverse species: all kinds of animals, plants, and fruit, the countryside, mountains that are crumbling, fearsome places that are terrifying to the viewer, gentle places that are mild and sweet with many colored flowering meadows swept with waves of soft breezes, streams that descend with the energy of great floods down from the mountain tops, sweeping with them great uprooted trees that fall pell-mell along with rocks, stumps, earth and foam, turning everything along the way upside-down. And there is the stormy sea, at odds with the winds, rising up in superb waves and then collapsing, crushing the wind beating against the waves, imprisoning it, and weakening it to break it in a mêlée of troubled foam. Thus it spends its fury. Sometimes, the sea is defeated by the winds, and it rises up over the banks of neighboring shores: splashing over the tops of hills as it descends down the valleys beyond. Some of the sea dissolves in

Leonardo da Vinci (1452-1519): Explosion on the Side of a Rocky Mountain. *(7 x 10-15/16 in.). Royal Library, Windsor.*

foam, some escapes only to fall back over itself as rain; some descends from the high cliffs to spread ruin, overturning everything it meets; sometimes it strikes an opposing force and then it rises up to the skies, filling the air with troubled clouds of foam. Then, thrown up again by the winds hiding in the nooks of the promontories it creates somber clouds dominated by the vanquishing wind".

Let's see what Leonardo is talking about. To find out, you will need a plaster-cast geometric figure, which you can either find in an arts supply store or make yourself by painting a box white. It is absolutely essential that your first constructions and studies of shadow are made by copying white geometric forms.

If you enjoy making things, you can construct plaster-cast forms yourself, using the following method.

For a pyramid shape on a triangular base, you will need a box and one-inch-wide masking tape. Using a ruler and a razor blade, cut three triangles of the same size from the sides of the box. Then go over the inside surfaces with turpentine, using a flat brush. Finally, tape the triangles together with masking tape to form the pyramid. Mix four cups of water with one cup of white glue, then add it to a bowl filled with plaster of paris, stirring the mixture as you go until it is about as dense as shampoo. Pour the plaster into the triangular mold, about three-quarters full. Be prepared: you will have to hold the mold upright for about thirty minutes, until the plaster is nearly set. Once this is accomplished, you can put a cardboard cover over the base and turn the mold right side up. Before you cover the base, however, brush the side of the cardboard that will be touching the plaster with turpentine and let it dry. Once the cover is affixed, turn the whole thing over in one quick movement and place it on a flat surface. After about half an hour, remove the cardboard. Because it was coated with turpentine, it should come away easily from the plaster cast. If you want to, go over the plaster with fine sandpaper to make the surface smoother.

Use the same method to make cubes, cones, and rectangles. You can even make a sphere by filling a rubber ball with plaster.

When you have collected several forms, arrange them on a dark flat surface and then focus a desk lamp or any other strong source of light to one side of the forms so they cast clearly defined shadows. Now, with a 2B pencil, begin to outline your forms on a piece of sketch paper.

Do not be afraid to erase — in fact, let me show you the best way to do this. Before the invention of erasers, artists used bread to erase their drawings and in Italy one may still be tempted to do this. Bread does a good job of removing finger-

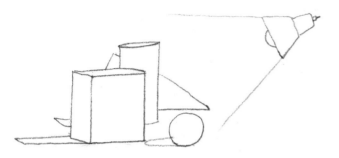

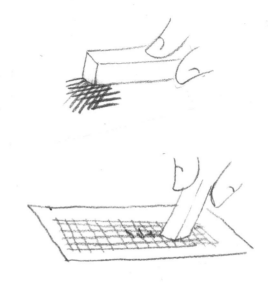

prints from the wall, but not from paper. The problem with bread is that it absorbs grease from your fingers and mixes it with the graphite in your drawing, so that after a couple of hours spent working on a composition you end up with grease marks all over your sheet, instead of erasures. Work only with an eraser and always keep it clean. If you want to get rid of a shadow that is too dark, press the eraser gently over the area you want to lighten. When you finish, look at the eraser. You will see that the part you used to erase with is now gray. To clean it, rub it over a clean piece of linen or cotton that you have stretched over a 6 x 8-inch wood frame for this purpose.

Continue to lighten and clean your drawing until you are satisfied with it. Remember only a clean eraser will give you the results you want.

To erase a line: rub vertically if it is a horizontal line; rub horizontally if the line is vertical.

If you follow this advice, you will avoid a dirty-looking drawing.

Now let's go back to our exercises. This time we will learn to draw a cube.

The first step is to draw the corner where the two sides closest to you meet in the foreground.

Next, note the point where the two sides of the opposite corner meet. Mark this point with a dot

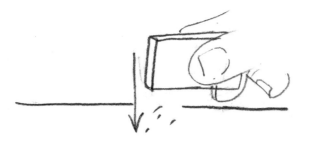

and then draw a straight line down from there. Mark the other two corners, taking care to keep them parallel to each other. Also mark the points at the base, keeping them the same distance from the first corner. Then connect all the points, even those that are unseen, the way I described in our exercise with onions. Once you have drawn the cube, erase the lines that are not seen and outline the shadows, trying to figure out their depth using geometric projection.

Once you have outlined the shadows, hatch them making long parallels strokes in one direction, then go back over the darkest area again, always in the same direction. Look at the areas in shadow and learn to pinpoint the darkest parts; in this case it is at the base of the side in shadows.

On the same sheet of paper, draw the same figure

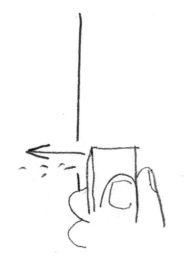

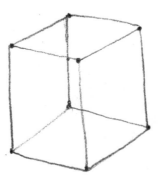

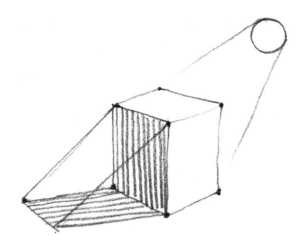

from different angles and move the light so it falls from different angles, to create different shadows.

Another way to fill in shadows is with crosshatching. In the past, the techniques of hatching and crosshatching corresponded to two separate schools, each considering the other's methods heretical. Hatching required the use of a rag or one's thumb to smudge the lines; this can be seen in the drawings of artists from the neoclassical period. Both schools produced very good artists. I do not wish to take one side or the other; I simply want to make you aware of both techniques. You can decide for yourself which one

you want to follow.

For your next exercise, place a sphere on a flat surface and spotlight it as you did in the previous exercise. With a 3B pencil, outline the figure and its shadow. Fill in the shadow with hatching at a 45-degree angle, then continue to hatch in the opposite direction. If you like, you can lightly smudge the lines with your finger or a stump before you begin the second round of hatching.

Now hatch again over the first lines, paying special attention to the darkest areas.

You should constantly refer back to your sphere with half-closed eyes, and occasionally hold your drawing away from you so you can see its faults. Be your own worst critic; it is the only way you will make progress.

For your next project, you might attempt to draw a decorated vase. When you have drawn its outline, trace the design on the vase with slightly

darker hatching than the vase's background. Be careful not to make it too dark; otherwise, it will end up looking more like a hole than a decoration.

As you are reproducing in black and white what is actually in color, refer to the tables on these two pages. They show how colors look in black and white.

Learning to reproduce shadows is fundamental, for shadows give a three-dimensional feeling to a drawing. Architectural manuals give precise rules for drawing shadows, but it is sometimes difficult to put these theories into practice when working directly with nature. Just remember that

Keep in mind that every color, if reproduced in black and white (by a photo or a movie camera, etc.), will result in gray of different intensities. I stress this point to encourage you to use these tables strictly, but also using the flexibility of your mind.

40

you should draw the shadows with the same care that you draw the objects themselves.

Compare Leonardo's studies of primitive and derivative shadows on page 42 with Pellizza da Volpedo's below, and you will immediately see how thoroughly these great artists studied the subject so that they could draw shadows correctly.

Pellizza da Volpedo (1868-1907): Solid Figures in Perspective. *Pencil, pen, and black ink, and with watercolors on white paper (18-3/4 x 26-1/4 in.). Private Collection, Milan.*

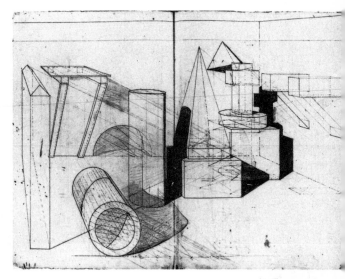

Every cold tone (green, blue, orange) has to be done using a lightly darker gray than the warm tones (red, yellow, orange). This because cold tones stress darkness and depth, while on the contrary, the warm tones point out the light and foreground.

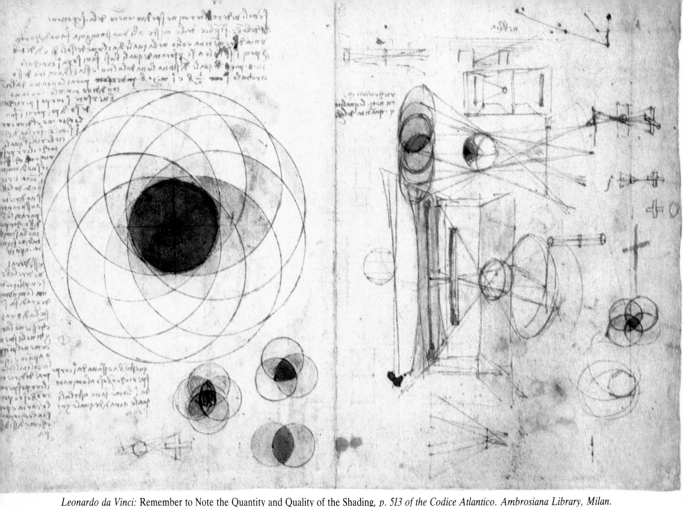

Leonardo da Vinci: Remember to Note the Quantity and Quality of the Shading, *p. 513 of the Codice Atlantico. Ambrosiana Library, Milan.*

Drawing Geometric Forms

Now we are ready to attempt a figure study with plaster-cast geometric forms so you can learn about the relationships between objects and their shadows.

For this study, you will need a bottle, painted white, as well as the other objects you have made or collected.

As you can see in the sketch below, the three other objects (apart from the bottle) have three very different shapes, and they can be repositioned and rearranged to fit within various imaginary geometric constructions.

When you arrange your objects, try to compose

them so they look harmonious. Do not leave this to chance; you should calculate everything carefully so the composition is pleasing to the eye.

Naturally, I did not invent these rules myself; they have been around for a long time and, in fact, have formed part of the curricula of art schools and studios since the Renaissance. Little by little, however, they have been neglected, until in the last twenty years they have been almost entirely forgotten.

A painter must store many different rules in his head and the best way to learn them is through experience and constant practice. In fact, it is the only way you can master the art and so be able to sketch, draw and paint in the way you want to paint. But the first step is always to work in a disciplined way and with determination.

Cennino Cennini, a painter of the late fourteenth and early fifteenth centuries, wrote in his *Book on Art*, chapter III: "What should one do to be successful? You whose gentle spirit gives you a love of virtue and who is destined for art, begin by clothing yourself in these garments: love, fear, obedience, and perserverance...".

You must draw constantly — keep a sketch pad and a soft pencil with you at all times. Record everything you see: monuments, animals, houses, trees, leaves — record it all. Do not ignore anything.

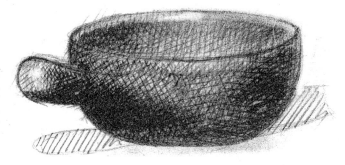

A Clay Pot as a Still Life

For this exercise, you must find a clay flowerpot in good condition to draw. As you draw it, look for its coordinates, referring to the sketches on the opposite page.

The ovals of the pots are all carefully constructed, but do not forget to draw the parts that are invisible as well. Later, you can erase them.

As you draw, be careful not to commit the typical error of trying to make the lines of the upper part and the base parallel. Be methodical in your construction, and, as you go along, you will find that gradually you are beginning to decrease the number of lines you need to construct an object. More and more often, you will be using your eye alone, which means you are learning to "read" the forms. Always keep the construction in mind, though, so you can verify that your drawing is correct.

To show you just how useful it is to make note of everything you come across, below are a few pages from my notebook. I sketched these small drawings from memory while I was writing the first draft of this book.

44

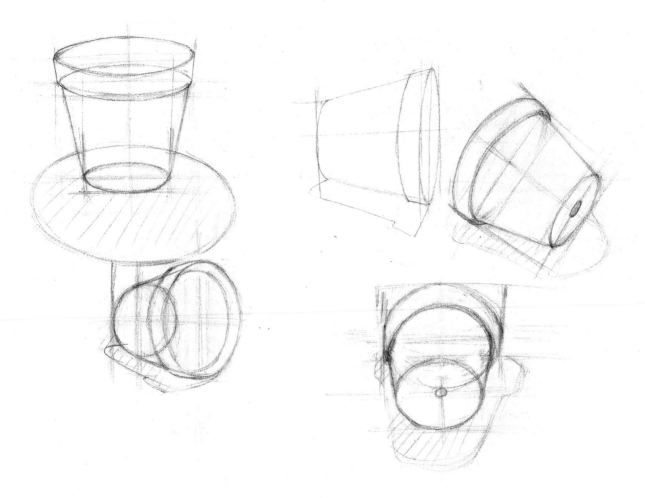

45

A Still Life from the Past

My drawing teacher had an amazing ability to assemble the most unlikely objects to create a composition. The most important thing to keep in mind when building a composition is harmony of shapes. For example, place a square object next to a round one, and an oval next to a triangle. Next to a vertical shape, place a horizontal one. Logically, if you have an object with a strong diagonal line going in one direction, you should put it next to another one with a diagonal line going in the opposite direction.

The drawing you see on the facing page is a rough sketch I did many years ago in an art class. Today I might do such a sketch with more precision because I have more experience.

The composition is seen from below, and on the wing of the bird you can see where my teacher has corrected my dark hatching.

The preparatory construction was done with care; I remember that I used a plumb line to avoid errors. Constructing a drawing was an obsession for me.

Once I finished the construction, I defined the areas in shadow with the help of crosshatching, covering the background with hatching at about a 20 degree angle. For this kind of drawing, begin with the background and then work on the figures and the different tones, keeping a rela-

tionship between each element, the depths of the shadows, and the quality of light and darkness. In a way, you must learn to paint with your pencil, and imagine that the different shades of gray are colors. Use your eraser to highlight areas that receive more light.

A Finished Still Life

As you can see, the drawing on the next page is more finished than the previous one. The relationship among the darker tones of the background, the lighter areas of the foreground, and the intermediate tones has been built up by degrees, by constantly comparing them with the objects next to them. Get into the habit of looking at your subject with your eyes half closed.

The drawing I have reproduced here, at an intermediate stage, was done with a 2B pencil to produce tones in various shades of gray. If I had continued with a 3B pencil I would very quickly have reached a shade that was too dark. At this stage, the light on the bottle is emphasized. The last and most difficult phase is hatching with a 1B pencil to give an illusion of roundness to the figures and to add the details.

To begin your sketch, lightly outline the contours of your objects with a 3B pencil. This outline

should be barely perceptible. To shade the background, work with the very tip of your pencil, always keeping a light touch, and then delicately smudge the lines with your index finger. With a very clean eraser, pick out the highlighted areas. Be diligent about keeping your pencil sharpened.

A Still Life and Some Hats by Pellizza da Volpedo

In my handbooks, I constantly mention Pellizza, whom I consider unjustly neglected by the public, and I urge my readers to learn more about his artistic achievements.

This still life composition by Pellizza of a table

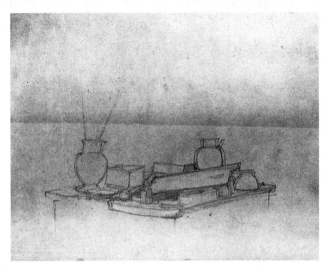

Above: Pellizza da Volpedo: The Painter's Table. *Pencil on brown paper (10-3/8 x 13-15/16 in.). Private collection, Tortona.*

with some objects on it is linear; the reason that the artist chose his table as a subject is probably because at the time he did it, he finally had his own studio which included a small table where he could leave his things. He must have been quite fond of the table because one day he drew it.

You can see his rigorous academic training in the drawing, evident in the double lines he has used

Left: Pellizza da Volpedo: Hats and Sketch for "Dit la Vérité?". *P. 19 of his notebook (average size of page: 4-1/16 to 5-11/16 x 5-15/16 in.). Private collection, Milan.*

in his outlines, implying a constant search for perfection. The drawing is dated 1888 and the artist completed it when he was only twenty years old. The study of hats shows what I mentioned previously — the importance of sketching everything around you from all angles. You should make many quick sketches to keep your hand and eye alert. After the first attempt, look at your subject again; your pencil should follow your eyes as you put what you see down on paper. As you gain experience, you will be able to draw your subject as you look at it, without having to refer constantly to the paper.

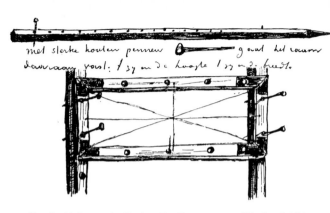

Van Gogh's Perspective Device. *The Hague, August 1882. Pen (2-3/16 x 4-3/8 in.). Fondation Vincent van Gogh, Amsterdam.*

Some Drawing Instruments
It is always a surprise to discover that even when such "antiestablishment" painters as the Impressionists drew and painted, they followed the same rules of construction that had been used since the Renaissance. There is an example of this in a beautiful letter from van Gogh to his brother Theo, in which Vincent speaks of a certain "perspective instrument".

"Dear Theo,
In my last letter you found a little sketch of that instrument for studying perspective. I have just returned from the blacksmith; he made iron points for the supports and iron corners on the frame. The instrument consists of two long poles; the frame is attached to them lengthwise or crosswise with strong wooden pegs. So on the beaches or in the countryside or in a field, one can look through it as through a window. The vertical and horizontal lines of the frame and the diagonal or intersecting lines, or rather, the division into squares forms certain points of reference. These help build a solid drawing, and indicate the principal lines and proportions. At least they do for someone who has some instinct for perspective and who understands why and how perspective gives an apparent change in the

direction of lines and alters the dimensions of the planes and the whole mass. Without this the instrument is of almost no use and looking through it makes your head spin. I think you can imagine how fine it is to direct this instrument towards the sea, towards a green field, towards a snow-covered field in winter, towards the fantastic network of thick and thin branches and tree trunks in the autumn or at a stormy sky.

Long and continuous practice with this instrument allows one to draw as fast as lightning — and once the drawing has been sketched out, to paint as fast as lightning too. In fact, this is just what one wants when painting; for the sky — the sea — the earth demand the brush, or rather, in order to express everything in a drawing, one must know and understand how to use a brush. I am sure that this will continue to strongly influence my drawings if one day I decide to paint. I already saw that in January, but then I had to stop and the real reason for this, besides some things of secondary importance, was that I was drawing without confidence. After that, six months have gone by and I have dedicated myself exclusively to drawing. And now, I begin again with new ardor.

The perspective frame is really a fine piece of craftsmanship. I am sorry you did not see it before you left. It was rather expensive but I had it made so solidly that it will last a long time. Thus, next Monday I will begin with some large charcoal drawings and use my frame and I will paint some small studies — and if they are good I hope that I will soon be doing better paintings.

I would like my studio to be a true painter's studio by the time you come back. You know that there were many reasons why I stopped painting in January, but that in the end you might say it was like the breakdown of a machine — a screw or a shaft was not strong enough and needed to be replaced by more solid parts.

I have just bought some strong warm trousers and as I had acquired a pair of sturdy shoes just before you arrived, I am now prepared to face the rain and storms. I am also determined to learn, as I paint landscapes, certain techniques that I think I need to know before going on to figures. For example, how to express certain subjects, tone and colors. In a word, how to express the body — the mass — of things. Your visit made this possibile, but before you came, a day did not pass when I did not think about it, only then I had to limit myself exclusively to black and white and to outlines. But now I have set sail. Goodbye, my friend, once again I send you a cordial handshake and remain,

Sincerely yours,

Vincent"

The perspective frame that van Gogh made resembled Leon Battista Alberti's "screen". This was an instrument portrayed by Alberti in his engraving *The Draftsman Drawing a Reclining Woman*. Van Gogh had seen many preliminary sketches executed by the great masters in which they divided their canvases into a grid. In an attempt to copy these painters, he had one made, using an old chair as the support. Between the two posts making up the back of the chair, he stretched horizontal wires and then wove vertical wires through them to make a transparent frame, through which he could look at his subject. The frame formed a grid, dividing his subject into small squares. Using these small squares as reference points he could transfer what he saw onto grid paper. This method of dividing a sheet of paper or canvas into squares was one that van Gogh probably took from the Dutch masters to whom he looked for his basic education.

Let's go back now and try to figure out how these Renaissance instruments were designed to enable an artist to draw perspective. Van Gogh had taken the idea from Albrecht Dürer (1471-1528) who in turn had learned it from Alberti, and from Leonardo during his stay in Italy, where he had gone to study perspective. The four engravings reproduced on these pages, in

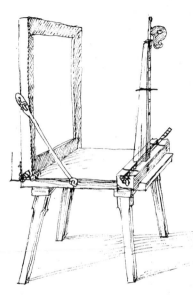

Above: Albrecht Dürer: Perspective Device, *1514. Preparatory drawing for the engravings in* Instructions for Measuring. *Nuremberg, 1525. Kupferstichkabinett, Berlin.*

Left: Albrecht Dürer (1472-1528): Man Drawing Reclining Woman. *Engraving from* Measuring Instructions, *printed in Nuremberg, 1525. Kupferstichkabinett, Berlin.*

Albrecht Dürer: Man Drawing a Seated Man. *Engraving from* Instructions for Measuring. *Nuremberg, 1525. Kupferstichkabinett, Berlin.*

which Dürer illustrates the basic concepts, are the fruit of these studies.

Here is how Leonardo used these instruments for drawing, as he explains in *Treatise on Painting*: "Have a large sheet of glass about half the size of a piece of good quality paper and affix it firmly in front of you so it is between you and the thing you want to portray; then stand back so that you are at a distance two-thirds of an arm's length from the glass, and use an instrument that will hold your head still so that you cannot move it. Then either cover or close one eye and with the brush or pencil trace on the glass what you see and then trace what is on the glass onto paper.

Above: Albrecht Dürer: Man Drawing an Amphora. *Right:* Man Drawing a Lute. *Engraving from* Instructions for Measuring, Nuremberg, 1525. *Kupferstichkabinett, Berlin.*

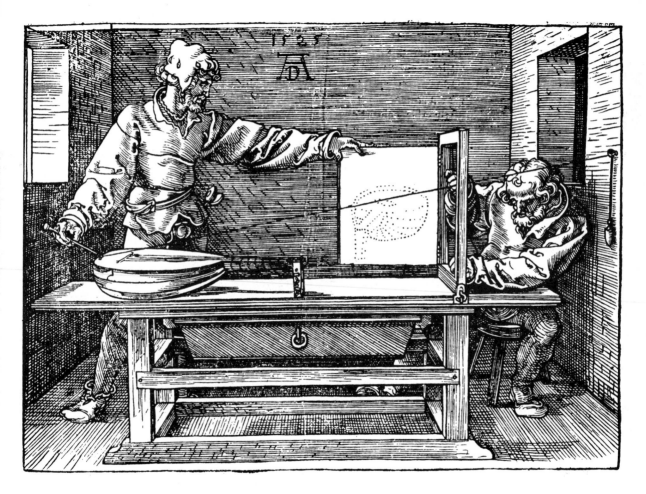

Leonardo da Vinci: Perspective Draftsman. *Codice Atlantico, 5th line. Ambrosiana Library, Milan.*

Now, transfer this to good paper and carefully paint it, if you like, using aerial perspective".

Leonardo has given a clear and simple definition of something which is actually quite complicated: that is, a drawing is nothing but the tracings on a vertical transparent surface (in this case the glass) of that which, if we stand still, is on the other side of the glass. Leon Battista Alberti substituted his "screen" for Leonardo's glass, and placed it between him and his subject. He explained how to use it in his treatise *On Painting*. Remember that you should not use these instruments for drawing before you have become skillful with your hand and your eyes. The instrument is only a help for those who are already skillful artists.

Pierre Bonnard Turns a Sketch into a Painting

The French painter Pierre Bonnard (1867-1947) was still a student at the University of Paris law school (where he, like several other painters, including Degas and Toulouse-Lautrec, initially studied law), when he decided to enroll at the Ecole des Beaux-Arts, and to attend the Académie Julian. There he met K.X. Roussel, P. Ranson, P. Sérusier, M. Denis, and E. Vuillard, artists with whom he formed a group called the Nabis, which favored a refined, intimate style of painting, in reaction to the Impressionists. These painters had studied the works of Gauguin, Degas and others, and, like the Impressionists, they were inspired by the Japanese prints that had been introduced in Paris in the 1870's andwere now to be found throughout Europe. Bonnard was the artist most interested in "Japanisme". Once he abandoned his polemic against Impressionism, his paintings took on more solidity, and his favorite themes (gardens, interiors, still lifes, nudes) were portrayed with naturalness, simplicity, and elegance.

Bonnard, who, besides painting, made lithographs and did decorative art, used a small agenda as a sketch book. Before he drew anything in it, he made a note of the weather of the day. You can see this in the sheet from it which I have reproduced on the next page. On it is written "Mardi 3 couvert" (Tuesday the 3rd, overcast). As he wrote these words, probably sitting at his breakfast table, he must have been attracted by the utensils used to make café au lait. Thinking it made a balanced composition, he decided to sketch it in his agenda.

Look at this little sketch and appreciate the beauty and confidence of the lines. Note, too, how the artist suggests volume and depth in a few light strokes.

For the person who works hard on construction

Pierre Bonnard (1867-1947):
The Coffee Grinder, *1930.*
Oil on canvas (18-7/8 x
22-7/16 in.). Private
collection, Winterhur.

Right: Pierre Bonnard:
Sketch from an Agenda.
December 3, 1929, showing
the preliminary drawing for
painting at left.

58

and practices constantly over a long period, sketches become a kind of calligraphy, an easy way of communicating emotions.

Now see how this small sketch jotted down on a few square inches of paper inspired a full sized painting. There is a lesson here, of which Bonnard is only one example.

I will let Bonnard finish this section in his own words: "I hope that my painting will endure and have no cracks. I would like to reach young painters in the year 2000 with the wings of a butterfly".

The Pencil Sketch

Painters should not limit themselves to formal studies while learning to draw. Get into the habit of taking notes, sketching everywhere you go, in city streets and on country roads. Carry a notebook and jot down everything that catches eye. Remember that it is very important to learn "to photograph" things with your pencil.

Looking again at both the sketch and the painting by Pierre Bonnard, I am struck by how much fresher in feeling a sketch sometimes is than a finished painting.

This is because a sketch is the result of instinct, an emotional reaction. A painting, on the other hand, is born of reason; it has been carefully thought out, all its details planned.

As you sketch, I suggest that you use grid paper at first so that you will have a sheet sub-divided into small areas.

Begin by sketching shapes that are familiar to you, everyday objects that you see around you. It should not be difficult to find subjects to be copied, start with the plant sitting on your table or the flowers outside your window.

The pottery mug with flowers in my sketch on the next page, looks as if it was been arranged by someone who knew how to compose both form and color harmoniously, this is what initially drew my attention. In the mug are branches of

rosemary, sage, forget-me-nots, and wild roses. It is important to know the names of the plants or flowers you are portraying, because each plant has its own character, and you should learn to express it. One painter who was a master of this was Paul Klee. Paul Klee was an artist whose main characteristic was the ability to capture the true essence of each form. Every line he drew on paper looks as if it occurred there naturally.

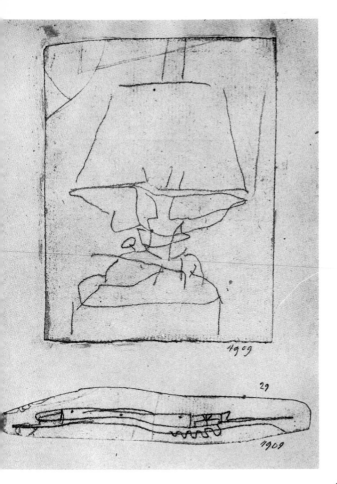

Seeing as Paul Klee Would See

Paul Klee (1879-1940) was the first painter to study children's art in order to learn how to look at an object with the eyes of a child.

A child does not draw what he sees, but what he knows and is familiar with. I do not want to get into a complicated discussion of the subject here, but to give you an idea of what I am talking about, here is a drawing of a lamp fashioned by Klee at the age of thirty, in 1909.

Klee constructed his drawings with a logic that was based on a fascinating theory, his *Theory of Form and Representation*, published posthumously in 1956. According to Klee, the line no longer represents the outer limits of a form and, consequently, it no longer represents the object. The line is something that is born, grows, and develops in a given space, as the seed of a plant grows in a given space. The painter no longer reproduces what he sees; instead, he invents on his canvas.

His was a fascinating and stimulating theory about which you can learn more by studying his works and writings. Here is an extract taken from *Creative Confessions*:

"Art does not reproduce what is visible; it re-

Paul Klee: Oil Lamp and Pocketknife, 1909. Pencil on Ingres paper (4-1/8 x 3-1/8 in.). Fondation Klee, Berne.

61

veals it. The essence of a drawing often and quite rightly leads to abstraction. In a drawing reside the fantasies and fairy tales of the imagination yet these are revealed with great precision. The more pure a work is, the greater is the importance attributed to the formal elements on which the graphic representation is based and the more deficient is the willingness to portray visible objects realistically.

The formal elements of a drawing are: the point, the energy of the line, the design, and space. An example of the element of design which does not let itself be broken down into smaller units: the energy coming from a pencil with a broad point, with or without modulation. An example of the element of space: the delicate misty shading spread with the brush, showing different nuances and density".

Let's try to read an object with the eyes of Paul Klee (and with the help of our pencils).

To do this, take a sheet of grid paper, and on it try to make an object "vibrate" by creating volume through the interplay of lines and emotions, through a process of association. For example, look at this drawing of a potted plant in flower and let me show you how I achieved it.

I began with the pot itself, which I reinforced on the right side with a vertical line perpendicular to the base, to render it more stable. I also drew

two almost parallel lines at the base, as if they were in perspective. The small plant grows up from inside the pot, then rains down from a cloud-like shape above, representing foliage. The foliage wraps itself around the flower, which represents the sun. Expressed very simply, this is seeing as Paul Klee would see.

Start making many exercises, working more with your mind than with the form you see in front of you.

A Still Life by Leonardo da Vinci

"Painting is mute poetry and poetry is a blind painting". This thought of Leonardo's seems appropriate for introducing a small study of his in sanguine pencil called *Oak Branch and Detail of a Plant Used in Dye-making*.

The heraldic nature of oak leaves and acorns (part of the heraldry of the Della Rovere family), led Leonardo scholars to advance a hypothesis that his drawing was a study for the garlands of plants in the lunettes over *The Last Supper* in the Refectory of Santa Maria delle Grazie in Milan or for some section of the decorations in the Sforza palace.

Look closely at Leonardo's drawing on the next page and notice with what delicacy, precision of form, and sensitivity to shadowing it was rendered.

Let's analyze the methods by which Leonardo achieved such shading. The acorn was defined using light hatching that followed the round form of the nut. The leaves in the foreground are shaded only around their veins, but the background leaves are shaded all over, with a second hatching along the veins. The background has been finished with uniform hatching at a 45-degree angle.

Let's try to copy Leonardo's drawing ourselves, imagining how a student of his would have approached it. The first time, copy it as closely as you can. Try to make it indistinguishable from the original. Use a pencil instead of sanguine (the technique is the same) on a piece of textured paper.

Once you have copied this study of Leonardo's, find a branch of your own with leaves and berries (or whatever you have around your house that is similar) and repeat the exercise.

Leonardo da Vinci: Oak Branch and Detail of a Plant Used in Dye-making. Red pencil on tinted red paper (7-7/16 x 6 in.). Royal Library, Windsor.

Drawing a Transparent Object

What could be more transparent than a light bulb? Let's look at how to draw one. I have divided the drawing into two parts to make it clearer. This way you can follow its evolution from the initial phase to the end. First of all, you must find a light bulb like the one in my drawing. Place it on a surface in front of you and look at it with half-closed eyes so that you get a sense of the variations of its tones. Begin by drawing the spherical part of the bulb, using the procedure I have taught you. Then sketch the axes of the light bulb, according to the way in which it lies. Sketch the form very lightly with a 2B pencil; use the grooved metal band at the bulb's end as a unit of measure. In my drawing, for example, the bulb is three times as long as the metal band and twice as wide. At this stage the drawing really begins. Continue the construction using the same reference points I have used.

Transparent objects always throw young painters, but I assure you that drawing them is much easier than it seems. You must learn to shade the areas in shadow progressively until you have rendered the darkest parts.

Do not get bogged down in the details, as so many beginners do, thereby losing sight of the whole. You will learn instinctively as you polish your artistic sensibility that the darkest areas make up the final touch of the drawing.

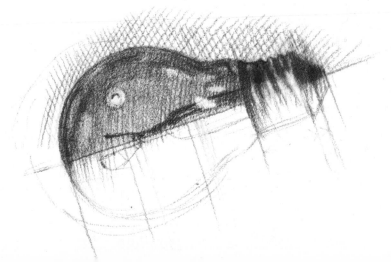

Camille Corot (1796-1875): Under Bush at Civita Castellana, *1826-27. Lead pencil (12-3/16 x 16-1/2 in.). Cabinet des Dessins, The Louvre, Paris.*

DRAWING LANDSCAPES

To help you understand the spirit with which you should approach nature, and the respect with which you should embrace it in order to draw it, let me quote from *Siddhartha* by Hermann Hesse:

"He looked around him as if seeing the world for the first time. The world was beautiful, strange and mysterious. Here was blue, here was yellow, here was green, sky and river, woods and mountains, all beautiful, all mysterious and enchanting, and in the midst of it, he, Siddhartha, the awakened one, on the way to himself.

All this, all this yellow and blue, river and wood, passed for the first time across Siddhartha's eyes. It was no longer the magic of Mara, it was no more the veil of Maya, it was no longer meaningless and the chance diversities of the appearances of the world, despised by deep-thinking Brahmins, who scorned diversity, who sought unity.

River was river, and if the One and Divine in Siddhartha secretly lived in blue and river, it was just the divine art and intention that there should be yellow and blue, there sky and wood — and here Siddhartha.

Meaning and reality were not hidden somewhere behind things, they were in them, in all of them".

Each aspect of a landscape is infinitely richer than anything the artist can portray in a drawing, but a good painter can at least express the emotion of what he finds in nature. The Impressionists, for example, were able to express their suffering through their interpretation of nature.

Let's begin with the tree, a subject that is rarely painted or drawn well these days — at least well enough to be easily recognizable as an oak, a pine, or an apple.

When looking at a modern painting, one sometimes wonders if the woods portrayed are made up of one kind of tree only, an occurrence that would be completely unnatural. Nevertheless, portraying the kind and character and charm of a tree in a drawing is difficult. We will therefore learn how to draw our trees in stages.

The mid-nineteenth century followers of Corot were very courageous when they decided to concentrate on landscapes, working from the village of Barbizon on the outskirts of the forest of Fontainebleau. Paul de Saint-Victor, an art historian of the period, expressed the conventional hostility to these painters:

"We prefer the sacred forests where woodland fauna roam to the forests where woodsmen work, Greek fountains where nymphs bathe to Flemish marshes where ducks splash, the semi-nude shepherd who leads his goats with Virgilian crook along Poussin's Georgic ways to the peasant who climbs Ruysdäel's path, smoking his pipe".

The images he uses in this extract may seem unbelievable at the end of the twentieth century, but in the middle of the nineteenth, his attitude was common. Those who commissioned and bought paintings were "refined people of good taste", and, as the director of the Beaux-Arts added contemptuously, referring to the Barbizon painters, "Theirs are the paintings of democrats, of people who do not change their underwear, who want to dictate law to good society; it is not art which pleases me; in fact, it disgusts me".

These words should help you better understand the situation of the painters of the Barbizon school, who at the time were considered mediocre artists, with no talent as draftsmen or colorists, and who were thought to attract attention and find buyers only because they were so extreme.

Camille Corot (1796-1875) was a man of natural generosity, and even though he did not want to take on regular students, he was always willing to receive beginners who approached him in his studio, and to give advice and suggestions.

Corot was really a very generous man. As an example, he gave a house as a gift to Daumier, the old and blind French artist who was dying in poverty.

He frequently said, "The first two things to study are form and values, two things which for me are the true fixed points of art".

Starting then with form and values, let us begin to draw some trees.

Form and Values

At the beginning, when you are just starting to draw, the most important thing you can learn is to "read" the form that you want to copy correctly. I have noticed in the classes I teach that one of the biggest mistakes beginners make when reproducing what they see is drawing things either too short or too tall, too wide or too narrow. They do not pay enough attention to getting the proportions of an object right or relating it to the things near it. They even draw curves that run contrary to the way they should go. These "faults" are seen by some to indicate a lack of talent for drawing, but in fact it is only a lack of experience in observing and "reading" a shape. I remember a phrase that my professor of frescoes used to say to me on this subject: "If you can write the letter 'o', you can also draw an egg". He was absolutely right. If you can form letters, you can draw because drawing is just a technique that everyone can learn, not different from writing, knitting or planing wood. It is a matter of transmitting to your hand the proper movements to be executed.

Let's consider values now, the tonal values as Corot understood them.

When we draw or paint, we have at our disposal only two dimensions — length and width — but the objects we want to reproduce are three-dimensional. We must therefore learn to render this third dimension of depth by creating an optical illusion, using not only perspective (a matter of form) but also, above all, values — the ample range of tonal values that shadows offer us, as we have seen in still life drawings.

Tonal value is very important in the study of trees. Thus, we must learn to read both forms and values.

Drawing a Fir Tree

In order to understand the form and tonal values of the fir tree, we must first see how the leaves are constructed. Try to obtain a branch from a fir tree and analyze its form closely, then begin to trace its axes and contour on a sheet of paper (fig. 1).

Inside this form, draw the small needles, giving a clear gray tone to the lighter ones and a dark gray cast to those that are in the shadows (fig. 2).

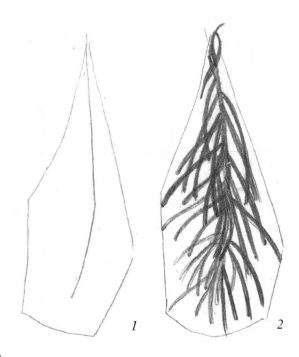

1

2

If you want to draw a detail of a fir tree from a middle distance, repeat the procedure you used before to draw the branch. Follow the movement of the branches, trying to read them through the green mass of the back-lighting, then draw the contours before going on to the lights and shadows (fig. 3).
The unusual structure of the leaves requires a kind of shading that is characteristic of the plant.

The kind of shading you see in the example (fig. 4) is achieved with hatching, using short strokes that constantly change direction. The darkest points should be the lower area of the foliage, which always remains in shadow.

3

4

Drawing a Tree Trunk

Following the method described, try to learn to read the form and tonal values of a tree trunk. The example given here (fig. 4) lets us observe the different phases of the drawing — the sketch of the form of the tree and the lines of the crevasses in the bark that gradually become darker with shading. If the highlighting and shading are done correctly, the tree trunk will appear to be round. You can carry out this exercise with a 2B pencil, following the techniques used to draw a sphere.

Remember, if you make some mistakes, do not use the bread eraser, because it absorbs grease from your hands and will grease your paper.

Two Drawings by Arnold Böcklin

Arnold Böcklin was born in Basel in 1827 and died in Fiesole near Florence in 1901. A painter with academic training, he was an able technician and excellent colorist.

Avoiding all contact with the major currents of the late nineteenth century, he developed a very personal and fantastic style of painting that anticipated surrealism.

Böcklin was above all a great draftsman — as you can see in the two drawings I have reproduced on the following pages.

Look at the way he has resolved the problem of the boundary of the fir forest in the first study. As he shows, you can paint with a pencil, in fact, you can even paint a canvas with pencils — color is just an extra element, as Ingres observed.

Böcklin observed the group of trees with half-closed eyes as he worked. Learn to read tonal values in this fashion; it is a basic rule for a landscapist to follow. You should also quickly learn to see which green should be in full light, where to put the lightest shadows (the half-tones), and the darkest ones. Find the areas of light and shadow on the trunk and learn to distinguish, evaluate and reproduce them.

Böcklin's second drawing offers us an example of the way to represent a single tree, perhaps a beech. In comparing the two drawings, you may notice that the artist has adopted two very different ways of depicting the foliage. Look at the outlines of the foliage — it is an important element to consider. Understanding form and volume is essential to becoming a good draftsman, along with, of course, constant practice.

In the second drawing, notice how he drew the whole tree before adding the highlights and shadows, following the same procedure he used with the firs.

It is absolutely important to copy from reality. If you have this handbook at your disposal, you can solve many difficulties.

Arnold Böcklin (1827-1901): Fir Trees, 1847. (16-1/8 x 11-1/8 in.). Hessisches Landesmuseum, Darmstadt.

Arnold Böcklin: Tree, 1850-57. (15-3/8 x 9-9/16 in.). Stadmuseum, Munich.

Drawing a Tree with Oval Leaves

To continue with our study of trees, I suggest another exercise. This one consists of copying a beech or some other tree with oval leaves.

The procedure is very similar to the preceding exercise: first, look at the tree as a whole, then get a leafy branch and analyze it carefully. Finally, try to draw it.

Construct the leaf (when fully developed it has prominent veining, a smooth matt surface and jagged edges) following the usual rules. Figure out the shading carefully, and do not forget to be very precise, because the more familiar you are with the details that you copy, the more at ease you will feel with your sketches.

When you reproduce a beech from a distance, you will notice that in order to give a sense of the volume of its foliage, and to suggest that it is made up of many small leaves that are blown by the breeze, you will have to define the leaves with undulating lines.

Try representing a part of the tree close up, as if you had a zoom lens that allowed you to focus on

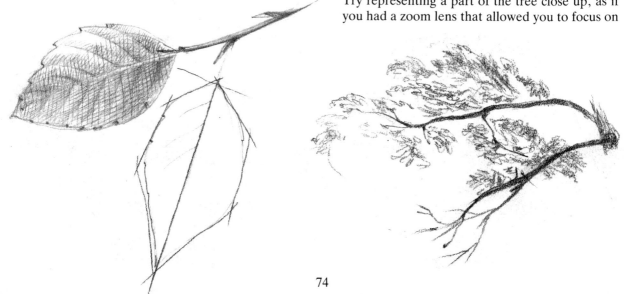

the details. This is a good way to do a study of an object.

To draw the tree in its entirety, first sketch it as a geometric form, then define its branches and, with a very sharp point on your pencil (use a 3B), try to suggest the existence of leaves using hatching and shading, being careful to render the volume of the beech's characteristically thick foliage.

Regularly check your drawing against your subject to verify that you are drawing what you see.

Do not draw trees like this.

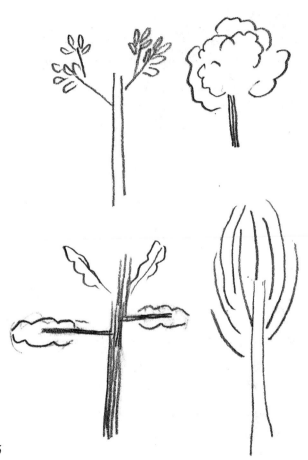

75

Trees are the most important elements in a landscape. A large tree in the foreground and a small one in the background immediately give a sense of perspective to a painting. A painting of a woods — whether it is one I have drawn or one drawn by someone else — always inspires a sense of peace in me.

Let's move on now to some famous examples of trees, drawn by artists from the Hague school of the late nineteenth and early twentieth century.

Willows at Heelsum by Willem Roelofs

Willem Roelofs (1807-1894) was one of the first among the Dutch painters of the Hague school to spend time with the painters of the Barbizon, the group I mentioned earlier. He may have become familiar with them through an exhibition of paintings in Brussels around 1850. Roelofs was also one of the first non-French painters to become interested in the kind of landscape paintings called "landscape portraits" and how to portray them, inspired by the members of this movement.

Roelofs quickly grew to appreciate the Barbizon school, for it had many things in common with the Hague school. The landscape as theme was common to both of them, though it had different origins.

Both schools looked at nature with wonder and were constantly surprised by what they saw. For this reason, their landscapes are immediate, quick, lively, and full of movement.

To show you what I mean, look at this drawing by Roelofs. I find it incredibly evocative.

Observe how the tree, with its contorted skeletal branches, seems to open and spread across the surface as if it were growing right out of the frame. The clever use of tonal values contributes to the dramatic nature of the scene by making the tree seem to vibrate. Who knows how many times you have stopped in front of just such a tree, one with a complex, imposing and tortured shape. The next time it happens, get out your notebook and try to "read" the form and tonal values of the tree. In this way, you will begin to develop the very important habit of drawing constantly, making notes of everything you come across.

Willem Roelofs (1807-1894): Willow at Heelsum, c. 1880. *(9-3/16 x 11-11/16 in.). Gemeentemuseum, The Hague.*

Anton Mauve (1838-88): Flock of Sheep. *(11-7/16 x 17-13/16 in.). Loaned from the Dienst Verspreide Rijkscollecties. Gemeentemuseum, The Hague.*

A *Flock of Sheep* by Anton Mauve

Along with Roelofs, Anton Mauve (1838-1888), a cousin of Vincent van Gogh and his first real teacher, also belonged to the Hague school.

Look at his drawing, reproduced here, of a flock of sheep in a meadow, which he drew with a soft pencil.

You will notice that the lines are similar to Roelofs'; later you will see a resemblance between Mauve and Frits Mondrian (Piet's uncle).

At the time that Mauve was painting, the Hague school was a breeding ground for new ideas, encouraging artists to develop a personal style of painting.

This was true of "schools", or artistic movements, in general. Their followers started with the same basic preparation, and just as Braque, Picasso and the Cubists had something in common, so did the Macchiaiolists, the Impressionists and the Expressionists.

Today we talk not of schools but of individuals. Remember, though, that an artist is the result of a process. If Paul Cézanne had not existed before him, Pablo Picasso might not have achieved such heights. The same can be said of Giotto in relation to Cimabue. One is not born a great painter, but becomes one, by assimilating the experience of the past, and by study, hard work, and sacrifice.

A *Village Scene* by Frits Mondrian

Here is another representative of the Dutch school, Frits Mondrian (1853-1932). The owner of a barbershop and wig store, Mondrian drew and painted for pleasure, often receiving advice from the painters who patronized his establishments. In 1890, he gave up the store to his wife to devote himself exclusively to drawing and painting. By 1907 he was a well-known painter, and his works were bought by collectors from the bourgeoisie and aristocracy.

When Frits Mondrian went to the Dutch flatlands to paint or draw, he often took along his young nephew, Piet, who grew up to become the famous abstract painter.

Let's look at Frits Mondrian's landscape (on the next page), drawn with a soft pencil. The first time I saw this drawing was at an exhibition in Milan in 1982. I was struck by how the artist achieved an extraordinary synthesis with just a few strokes to shape the outlines (form), and hatching to give it volume (tonal values). It has both a strong foreground and background, giving it a feeling of depth. The reflections in the water give it a feeling of stillness, with no hint of wind to disturb it. The drawing expresses the peace and light of summer — if you look at it with half-closed eyes you will be able to see what Frits saw.

80

The painter probably used a 4B pencil and did the whole painting at one sitting. Look at the way he drew the tree trunks, shaping them with just a few strokes to suggest their solid structure. I recommend that you take a trip to the countryside, too, and that you take this book with you. Look for landscapes that resemble Mondrian's, with trees and dwellings reflected in the water. Keep the book open and turned to this page as you work, and try to copy your subject using this drawing as a reference.

Autumn Landscape by **Piet Mondrian**

Piet Mondrian is best known for his abstract paintings, but his early work was more academic in style. This was the result of the rigorous early training his father had insisted on so that Piet might become a drawing professor. His brother, Carel, describes the era (1886): "The old room where we played as children had been transformed into a studio and Piet studied there. I can still see him arriving home with an enormous cast of Moses' arm or various plaster-casts, like the head of the Laocoon that he would borrow from school in order to do charcoal studies. He studied perspective, the stylization of flowers and plants, and, from books, anatomy. Nor did he overlook art history. It was all part of the exams. But neither father nor Uncle Frits could teach him what he needed to know to pass his exams: he had to do that by himself".

Uncle Frits had given Piet his first lessons in painting and, in particular, suggestions on how to depict a landscape. But, by 1909, when his nephew's paintings were beginning to be noticed in Amsterdam and had provoked comment from the press, Frits had distanced himself from Piet and his painting, claiming that their work had nothing in common.

After three years at the Academy and two years of evening classes in Amsterdam, Piet Mondrian was only just starting to work. At the beginning, his life was not easy; to earn a living he had to do all sorts of work, from illustrating books, to making copies in museums, to giving classes.

Piet was strongly attracted to the Dutch countryside and took inspiration from simple motifs, such as the silhouette of a windmill, cows in a meadow, a farm in the middle of fields, reflections in the water, etc.

Frits Mondrian (1853-1932): View of a Village. (16-1/8 x 8-7/8 in.). Private collection, Haarlem.

The landscape reproduced here was done by Mondrian around 1902-1903. It was the work of the mature artist, produced with great freedom of line; however if you compare it with the other landscapes on earlier pages, you will find a resemblance — there are still traces of earlier influences.

When a painter becomes a master of the art, he prefers to draw with very soft pencils: by varying the pressure he uses, he can vary the thickness and lightness of his lines. This is something a harder pencil does not allow.

The feeling evoked by the drawings we have been studying is one of peace, a sensation that is hard to find in paintings now.

Drawing Houses

For the past several years, I have found it more and more difficult to draw a landscape. One has to travel farther and farther in order to get away from the modern architecture that is destroying the land. Taste in architecture these days is horrendous. Our towns, our cities and even the countryside are full of horrible structures. In par-

ticular, housing developments and seaside resorts with thirty story buildings overlooking the water are truly disturbing landscape elements. The only thing to do is to go deeper into the country seeking out the hamlets and villages that are still untouched. The buildings may be a bit ramshackle, but they are better than the newer ones in the city centers.

The Château at Amboise Seen from Clos-Lucé by Leonardo da Vinci

This drawing, in sanguine pencil (or as some call it, red pencil), has given rise to a great deal of controversy about its authorship. Some specialists say that since it was done with the right hand, it could not have been executed by Leonardo, who was left-handed (in fact, he was ambidextrous). I have always wondered how a right-handed drawing is distinguished from a left-handed drawing. It seems a bit like the coffee mug invented for left-handed people.

In accordance with this theory, the drawing has been attributed by some to Melzi, who was Leonardo's favorite student. Melzi accompanied him to France and, as history books tell us, he approached the technical excellence of his teacher: "...this drawing is almost certainly by Melzi whose study of the head of Ambrosiana, dated 1510, shows how well he could imitate Leonardo

Piet Mondrian (1872-1944): Autumn Landscape. *Herbstlandschaft, c. 1902-03. Gemeentemuseum, The Hague.*

Leonardo da Vinci: The Château at Amboise seen from Clos-Lucé. *Red pencil (5-1/4 x 10-3/8 in.). Royal Library, Windsor.*

in his usage of the red pencil...".

I would like to digress on the subject of the term imitation and its significance in Leonardo's time. Melzi did not imitate in the sense that we understand it today. What he did was try to draw as well as his teacher, carefully studying how Leonardo drew so he could learn his methods. This was the only way to work as part of Leonardo's studio, and it was a mark of pride for the student. Leonardo said, "It is a sad student who does not go farther than his teacher". And to go farther than the teacher, one had to learn to draw like him.

Look now at this drawing of a landscape, and think about it entirely from the point of view of esthetics and execution.

Forget about who drew it.

If one observes the drawing in its details: the château, the houses, the bridge, the lay-out, the strokes, and the age of the paper, one feels that it is a painting of a bygone era, of time lost forever. The drawing could also have been done with a black pencil — I chose it not for its technique, but for its subject and the atmosphere it evokes. When you draw a landscape, you might try using the instruments that I described to you earlier in the book; they are still used by great painters today. You will find they will make your job much easier.

The Pencil Sketches of Edgar Degas

Edgar Degas loved Italy. He had a sister living there and when he visited her, he took full advantage of the countryside. Like all painters, he sketched endlessly in the travel notebooks he carried with him in his pockets so he could jot down his "impressions".

The small, delicate sketch that you see reproduced on the next page gives a strong sensation of light, and if you compare it to that of Leonardo (or Melzi as the case may be), you will see that the difference between them is not great, even though 350 years separate the two drawings.

The impressions Degas committed to paper with his pencil are further explored in his writings. Here is what he wrote during a trip to Rome and Florence in 1858:

"Returned to the chapel [the Mazzatosta chapel in Santa Maria della Verità in Viterbo] of Lorenzo da Viterbo. Truly superb, striking heads. ...

Followed the ramparts to Paradiso. Jean Sebastian del Piombo. It is surprising how it resembles Avignon.

Ten p.m. Left for Orvieto. Moonlight. I could distinguish the countryside and the mountains. Superb land. Montefiascone. Mountains. The sun rose, haze covering the plain — we went down to the Orvieto valley. The dome appeared above the haze. Climbed the ramps, a real eagle's nest. The White Eagle (the name of a hotel in Orvieto). ...

Sublime dome, I was completely staggered. Façade, full of richness and taste. The mosaics were too new. One with a terrible decadence. I recognized some sculptures. I entered and ran to Luca Signorelli.

It always happens that in the most beautiful monuments there is such a mixture of tastes. I recognize well this beauty of the famous seraphins [by Signorelli]. I do not know what to say. I am in a dream that I can not recall.

Subjects from Dante, ingenious, thrilling; a kind of raging arabesque; the contrast of movement and a love for stirring things up that is Luca Signorelli with the peace of Beato Angelico who is here, especially his Christ, more beautiful than ever [a fresco of a majestic Christ by Fra Angelico]. Ah, Michelangelo's man is good [Signorelli].

I went around the church. Returned to the hotel bathed in sunlight. Slept until noon. Dinner. Wrote to Uncle Achille.

Went to the wells of St. Patrizio. ...

A superb view of the door of the fortress above the valley with the Tiber in the background. Went to the dome. Started a drawing of a seraphin. Someone was playing La Traviata loudly on the organ. What a mockery. Walked along the ramparts. All through the streets with houses from the Middle Ages.

The sun behind Mt. Cimino. ...

I do not feel like going to draw from nature, Luca Signorelli holds me enthralled. I must think about figures above all else or at least study them thinking only of the background.

Night, six o'clock at the church, back at four, walked towards seven to the Citadelle. ...

Near the wells [of St. Patrizio] I looked at the plain. Superb sight, something to remember for a lifetime. ...

The Tiber is dry and the sun sets next to the road to Florence. All the beautiful planes of the mountains. The most beautiful moment of the day?

I think of France which is not as beautiful but my love for home and for work in some little corner still gets the better of any desire I might have to enjoy this lovely bit of nature forever. ...

There are some pretty women and girls here. It is the Florentine charm. Still a bit of Roman savagery.

... Supper. The bother of departure. Left for Perouse in rain and lightning. (1 ecu, 80) We were in the mountains, we went up and down —

Edgar Degas: Landscape, *1856. Pencil (7 x 9-3/4 in.). Cabinet des Dessins. The Louvre, Paris.*

moonlight. July 29th. This morning at 5:30, arrived at Città della Pieve on a small rise, in a pretty plain, surrounded by mountains with some white clouds at the tops. At the cathedral, a fine Perugina behind the altar. ...

A church outside a port [St. Agostino]; at the right when you enter a lovely tableau from the Ecole de Francia. It is like being in the countryside around Naples, the land is so fertile and cultivated. ...

Returned to the hotel, spent the day feeling tired and not knowing what to do. Wrote to Rouget. ... At 4:30 I walked along the lake. This lake is the lake of Chiusi [?]. It is stormy in the distance. To travel alone you must go to places that are either very lively or full of art. Boredom quickly overcomes me when I contemplate nature. Always some priests out for a walk. All the women look like a Perugino. Is this an illusion?

Finally at 10 p.m. left for Perouse. ... Arrived in Perouse at 4:15, drawn by oxen up the rise to Perouse. ...

Magnificent effect, 2 lines of pilgrims crossing the main street in front of the the governor's palace, singing and going to sit on the steps of the cathedral. ...

It is barely daylight. The pretty tones of the figures sitting on the steps. ...

The old palace. Very tall. It is necessary to draw the whole thing right up to the top to render the space around the figures.

... Hotel de la Corona. At 8:30 I started to run".

Drawing a Landscape: Perspective

To draw a landscape, you must first understand how to look at what you want to draw. The eye embraces a circular "visual field", restricted by the pupil and elongated towards each end. This phenomenon is best represented by a cone. The visual cone has as its main axis a line going from the pupil to the center of the circle at the

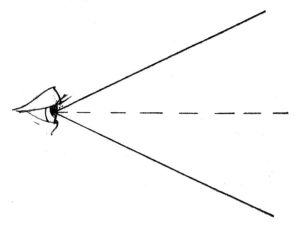

wide end of the cone. The two opposite generating lines of the cone that show the limits of the field of vision form an angle of about 50 degrees.

When you draw something on a sheet of paper, the paper being ideally placed between the subject and your eye, you should always draw it

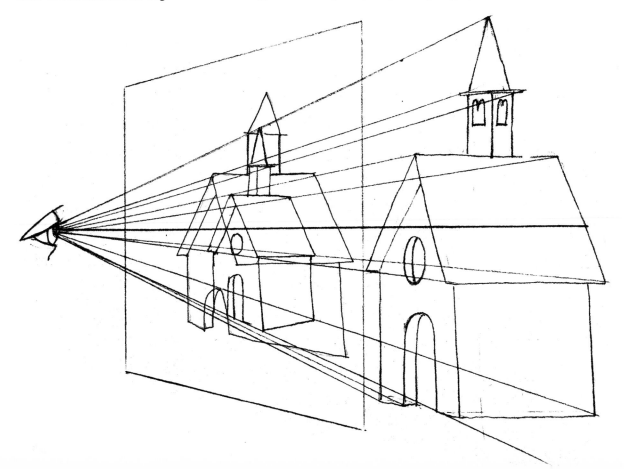

smaller than your whole field of vision; otherwise your visual cone can not take it all in.

If the area of your drawing is greater than an aperture of 50 degrees, it will end up with an

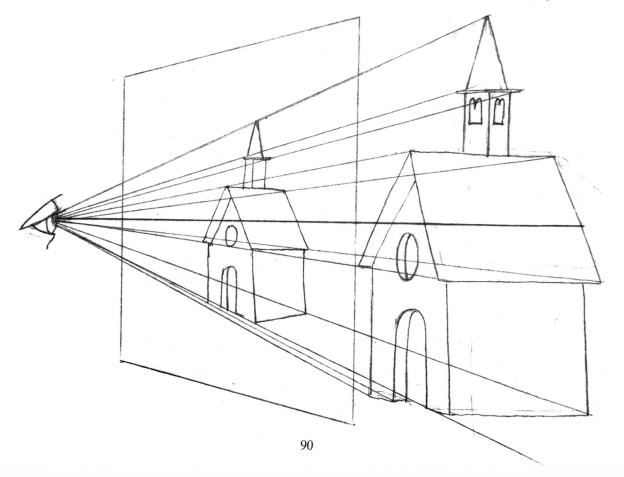

altered perspective.

The point where the lines seem to converge is called the "vanishing point", and it is always placed at the observer's center of vision.

into the country, taking your drawing material and this book. Look for a group of houses that resemble the ones on page 93.

Begin by drawing the horizon and the vanishing

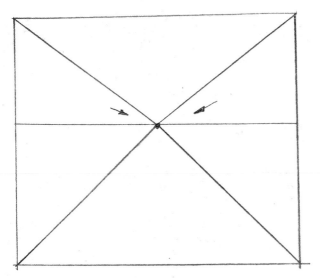

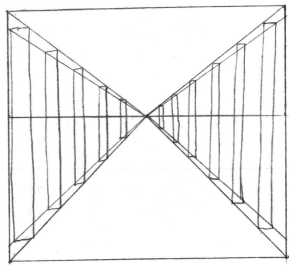

Objects seem to get smaller as they get farther away from us (think of a colonnade or a line of street lights). Let's see how this works.

To do this exercise properly, you must go out

point towards which all the parallel lines converge. Draw a rectangle, the first surface of the façade of the house, then extend the lines from the four corners towards the vanishing point.

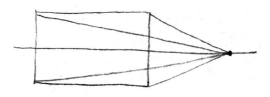

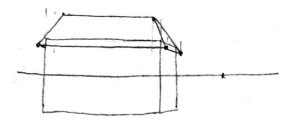

Then, locate the depth of the side of the house to the right of the façade.

After you have drawn the façade of the house, you can add the roof. Use dots to indicate the

sharp pencil, connect these points.

The windows should be aligned horizontally and vertically, and should be equidistant. Draw the

lines of construction, then outline the windows, adding shadows and highlights.

The trees in the background reach a fixed height

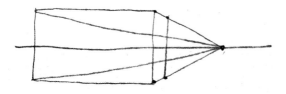

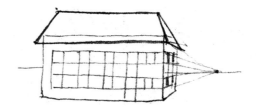

point where the roof extends beyond the façade and its highest point. The highest point should be recessed from the line of the house. This will also determine the angle of the roof. With a soft

corresponding to where the horizontal and vertical lines of the house intersect. The trunks are almost at its base. Draw the trees in as I described in the last chapter.

If your first drawing does not look just the way you would like it to, do not be discouraged. Just start again — eventually you will succeed.

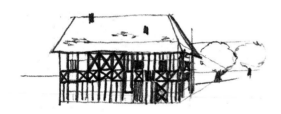

The Metamorphoses of Arnold Böcklin

Let's continue exploring the many possibilities of the drawing pencil. This time we will see how an artist can be inspired by a landscape and transform it into something completely different. Look at Böcklin's drawings on the next page. They are striking proof of my earlier point about pencil drawings being anarchic and creative. The transformation was completely done with

pencil; only the final work was copied in oils.

Note the first drawing in the sequence. It is a landscape with trees and rocks, shaped with a soft pencil. The artist has changed the frame of the drawing after finding a better way to balance it, a good habit to get into as you use your notebook. Choosing a frame for your composition is very important.

In the second drawing of the rocks, he has begun to change them into two grotesque figures. By the third drawing, he has added an eye in the large white rock on the extreme right.

If you look at the eye and try to work out what figure it belongs to, you will discover the head of a hare in profile. A bit of ear extends above the eye, and the tip of the nose ends just above the smaller rock, which has now been turned into a man walking.

In the last drawing, the metamorphosis is complete. One can clearly distinguish two figures leaning against each other. They remind me a bit of Don Quixote and Sancho Panza.

The sequence does not end here, for there are endless drawings and variations. These examples give you an idea of the way to proceed with this kind of exercise. As you draw, you can create and transform to your heart's content; you do not just have to copy.

In the next chapter, we will concentrate on the

1   2

Arnold Böcklin: Study for a Landscape (Tree and Rocks). *1851. (5-7/16 x 4-1/2 in.). Kupferstichkabinett, Basel.*

94

3

4

figure: how to compose it and how to frame it on a sheet of paper; how to choose the right pose for your model and how to draw such details as the eyes, nose, mouth and hands.

Egon Schiele (1890-1918): Reclining Nude with Raised Left Leg. *1914. Pencil (12-1/2 x 18-7/8 in.).*

DRAWING THE FIGURE

Great painters have always followed strict rules for constructing the figure. In the past, art academies were highly demanding of their students, and many young artists felt the constraints of their methods. This often provoked the most avant-garde among them to criticize and rebel against such traditional training.

It should be remembered that the mission of these art schools was to train students for a craft, and this was only possible if very rigorous methods were used.

James Ensor (1860-1949), a Belgian painter, referred to his academic studies as "healthy years of slavery". This may have been true of the teaching methods of the past, but today students are left much more on their own. Nevertheless, it is important to remember that for drawing as well as for painting, it would be impossible to create something new if we did not have the experiences of the past. Even the happiest inspirations are based on what has gone before.

A Woman by Egon Schiele

Egon Schiele (1890-1918) was the beloved student of another great master, Gustav Klimt, whose influence can be seen in Schiele's work. Klimt had a strong effect on Schiele, who died young, before he was entirely free of his teacher's authority. But I do not think it is always bad to be inspired by a good teacher (think of Leonardo and his pupil Melzi). The problem comes when one imitates someone mediocre.

During his student days, Schiele was already searching for something different, which he seems to have found in Klimt.

Study the female nude reproduced here and you will see Klimt's influence on Schiele. Let's look at it in detail. The first resemblance to Klimt that you may notice is in the position he chose for the model, and the shape the composition takes on paper. Yet, the contour lines, or tracings, as they are sometimes called, which are so characteristic of a painter, are not like Klimt's at all. At first glance, these lines may seem to be an interpretation of Klimt's lines, for they are hard and hint at a neurotic personality. But Schiele has added a touch of softness to his drawing by repeating a series of short strokes in the shaded areas.

The pose itself is quite provocative, and the overall outline of the drawing accentuates this.

Now look at the composition. The geometric

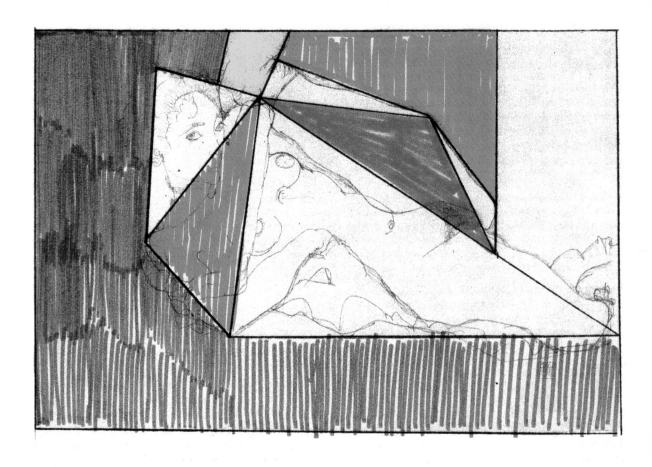

structure that sustains the figure is made up of a series of triangles.

If you draw these triangles on a piece of tracing paper and then copy them onto a blank sheet, you will see the rapport between the enclosed areas of the figure and the empty spaces of the background. If you then fill in the triangles yourself with different tones of grey, you will discover an abstract composition that recalls the paintings of the French painter, Serge Poliakoff (1906-1969).

This artist paints abstract paintings, and his geometrical approach is very original and recognizable.

During his short life, Schiele was accused of corrupting minors and distributing obscene drawings for which he spent a month in prison. Considering how moral standards have changed in our time, and considering what can be published today, Schiele's drawings, in comparison with much that is published today, show a remarkable talent and genuine affection for his model.

Male Nude, Lying on His Back by Gustav Klimt

The era of Klimt (1862-1918) and Schiele was also the era of Freud, Kafka, Hesse and Hitler. This last was one of many students rejected by the art school in Vienna that Schiele attended. It has often struck me that if Hitler had been accepted by the school, we might have had one more painter and one less dictator, and the course of history would have been very different. This reminds me of a comment by Blaise Pascal: "If Cleopatra's nose had been shorter the whole history of the world would have been different".

In 1897, Klimt was one of the founders of the Vienna Secessionist movement, an artistic movement that arose in opposition to traditional art and rapidly became the dominant force. During his life Gustav Klimt also approached the Expressionist current and from 1907 was in contact with the two principal Austrian representatives of the group, Oskar Kokoschka and Egon Schiele.

An extraordinary academic draftsman, Klimt rapidly became a great success. The drawing on the following page was done when he was only eighteen years old, but it displays in its composition and sure lines the high level of academic training he had received.

Before drawing from live models, Klimt would have needed a thorough grounding in basic techniques, which would have included the study of the bone and muscle structures and drawings from plaster-casts. Without such preparation, it would have been difficult for him to have reached such a high degree of figure drawing skills. Only a

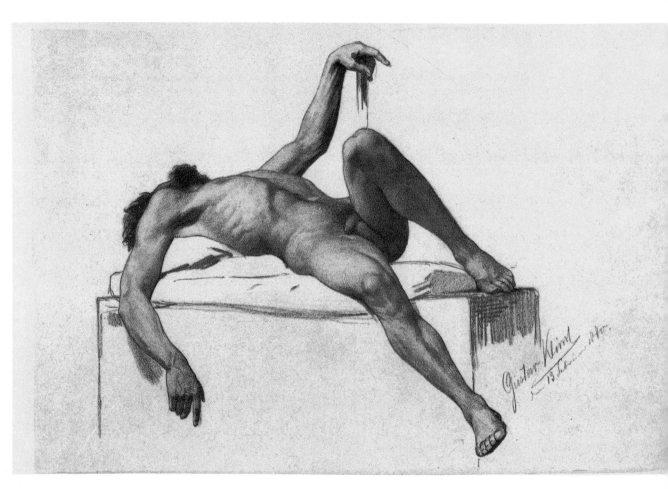

few exceptional cases, such as some of the Impressionists painters, have been able to do without such training.

Looking at this drawing, it is difficult to think that this was made by the same Klimt who painted those tormented figures that we all know.

Drawing the Figure: Proportion

Let's look in detail at the necessary stages of figure drawing.

It has been established that Polykleitos's statue of the Doryphoros, a Greek sculpture from the fifth century, B.C., familiar to us from copies in museums in Berlin, Florence and Naples, has the perfect figure.

Look at the charts on the next page showing drawings of the skeleton as seen from different angles. These studies should be copied as accurately as possible. Try to find a good book on anatomy for artists or, alternatively, visit a natural science museum where you can sketch skeletons that you can later complete at home.

Gustav Klimt (1862-1918): Male Nude, Lying on His Back, 1880. Pencil (11-3/8 x 17 in.).

Right: Sketch of the Doriphoros, A statue by the Greek sculptor Policletus, drawn by Luisella Lissoni.

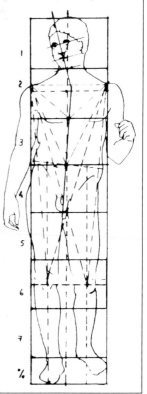

The Figure in Proportion

From Vitruvius, we measure the human figure in multiples of the head.

Here are the proportions of the ideal figure: the total height is seven and a half times the length of the head; the width of the shoulders is twice that of the head; the neck is half a head long. The whole body is measured this way, as you can see in the chart.

Once you have understood and memorized this rule, we can begin our studies.

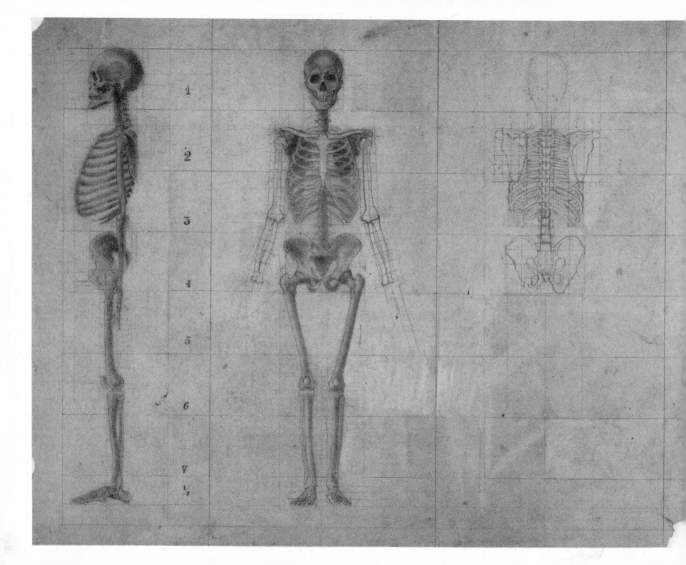

1

2

3

4

5

6

7

½

I also urge you to find reproductions of the drawings of the great masters of the past, especially Leonardo, and copy them, trying to imitate the construction, the light, and the shadows.

The next step is to study the muscles of the body. This also requires a certain amount of zeal. If you can, enroll in an anatomy class. If this is not possible, the next best thing is to learn to copy plaster-casts and statues, and then the drawings of the great masters. It is the only way to learn the muscle structure.

Look at the anatomy study drawn by one of my old schoolmates, Giorgio Balconi. His work is the result of at least a month of practice and was made on cartridge paper; the hatching was done with a 3B pencil, the shading with a 2B and the detail work with a 1B.

On the next page there is a pencil copy of Botticelli's *Birth of Venus*, drawn by Degas. Degas worked from an easel placed just the right distance from the drawing. If you should have the chance to copy a reproduction, try to get one that is at least poster-sized. Hang the picture from a wall and work standing up, from your easel, and not at a table.

While he was still learning his craft, Degas tra-

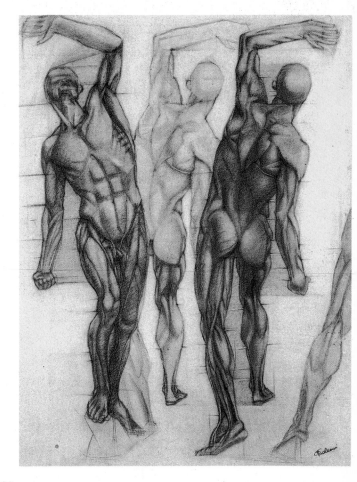

Giorgio Balconi: Anatomy. *The artist's collection.*

velled several times to the south of France and to Italy (between 1854 and 1860), and his notebooks of that period are devoted to one of his greatest passions, the history of art. There were many reasons why Degas copied from the old masters, but the main one was to create a repertoire of subjects and compositions to inspire him in the future.

Cézanne, similarly, often went to the Louvre to copy the drawings and paintings of old and contemporary great masters. John Rewald, the Cézanne's scholar, wrote: "The problems that Cézanne confronted in drawing at the Louvre were his own special problems. He did not attempt faithful reproductions of his subjects. What he wanted to do was to penetrate the movement that made them come alive, to note the essential lines in his sketchbooks and to indicate lightly the shadows that made them three-dimensional".

Left: Edgar Degas (1834-1917): The Birth of Venus, after Botticelli. *1859. Pencil (11-13/16 x 8-7/8 in.). Collection of Madame Feichenfeldt, Zurich.*

Right: Paul Cézanne (1839-1906): Copy of the Lycian Apollo from An *ancient statue in the Louvre, 1881-84. Pencil (8-1/4 x 4-3/4 in.). Kupferstichkabinett, Kunstmuseum, Basel.*

Paul Cézanne: The Nymph, after Pierre Julien. *1882-85. (8-1/4 x 4-13/16 in.). Kupferstichkabinett, Kunstmuseum, Basel.*

***Female Nude on Her Stomach* by Gustav Klimt**

This female nude was drawn by Klimt when he was forty-three, many years after the earlier academic drawing we saw. The figure is drawn in profile and sketched in the characteristic way that so influenced his contemporaries.

The drawing is rendered with delicate lines that are sometimes drawn double, giving a peculiar vibration to the figure. The work, like all Klimt's work, is reduced to the essentials: the line is slightly stronger only in the areas in shadow. One can also see evidence of Ingres's theory that line itself is sufficient to evoke emotion; shading and color are extra.

The Model's Pose

Drawing a pose from memory is another important exercise. First, outline the bone structure as you imagine it; then add the contours. Lastly, have a model actually take that position in order to check your drawing. Naturally, you will have to correct and perfect it. Do not leave your poses up to chance, but try to follow a geometric structure, using the great masters as inspiration.

Gustav Klimt: Female Nude on Her Stomach. *1905-06. Pencil (14-1/2 x 22 in.).*

107

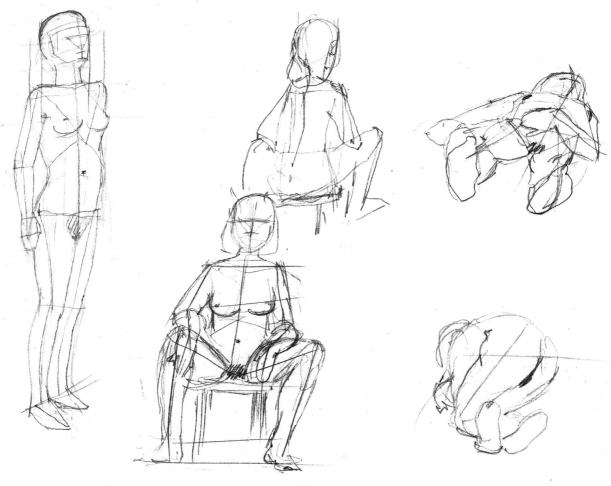

108

Female Nude, Lying on Her Back by **Degas**

The splendid nude by Degas on the next page, achieved with a graphite pencil, falls into the category of great drawings. One is struck right away by its impressive construction and the delicate use of light and shadow. The composition and pose are rather unusual, contradicting earlier rules of composition associated with the nude. Let's read one of Degas's notes referring to another drawing, as collected by George Moore:

"Up until now, the nude has always been portrayed in poses that presuppose a public looking at it, but my women are simple honest women. Here is one — she is washing her feet. It is as if you were looking at her through a keyhole".

The relationship with his models is another important activity of the painter.

The poses that you have your models assume should be studied and calculated so that they are not too tiring, for they will, naturally, need to move. You should not expect them to hold poses for more than twenty minutes at a time. When it is time for them to rest, do not forget to mark an outline of their feet with a piece of chalk if they were standing, or, if they are sitting, the position of their hands or buttocks, so they can return to the same place.

Let's read about a modeling session from another of George Moore's extracts on Degas.

"My God! You are really posing badly today" cried Degas to his model as she banged his fist on a stool. "If you are tired, say so".

"Yes, I am tired," admitted Pauline, who after a moment, made a last effort to balance herself again on her left leg, while with difficulty she held her right foot raised behind her with her right hand.

"Well, then, rest a moment. Afterwards, try harder with that pose".

With a frown, the young girl slipped her bare feet into the slippers lying next to her and came down from the modeling table without a word. She went over to the stove and there she rubbed her legs, swollen from holding the difficult pose. From time to time she glanced in irritation at the old artist who continued to model his statuette. Why did he have to scold her all morning? "You must do better than that!" "Raise your leg more!" "Keep your body straighter!" "Don't get sloppy!" Hadn't she been doing her best to pose the way he wanted? And why didn't he talk to her when usually he was so talkative? Every time she tried to start a conversation, he replied in monosyllables. And then there was his poor old servant whom he had scolded that morning in such a harsh way, on the pretext that the fire was not lit properly, so that she was reduced to tears.

"Did you have a pleasant walk yesterday, monsieur Degas?"

"Yes, quite pleasant. I took the tram to Pigalle up to porte de Vincennes. When I got there, I walked a little to the fortifications, then I took another tram to Saint-Augustin. From there, I came back on foot, quite leisurely".

"That's quite a stroll! It's farther than your walks to Montmartre".

"That's quite true!... This afternoon, I may go to Montrouge and tomorrow to Auteuil or somewhere else. Or I may just get on the first tram that passes by and ask the conductor where we are going... When I have explored every neighborhood in Paris, I will again take up my pilgrimages through Montmartre, for I still like it best. At least there I know all the streets and don't have to ask anyone for directions... But when it comes down to it, it doesn't matter much where I walk because my poor old eyes no longer distinguish anything anyway".

"It is not very wise of you to walk like that all alone," said Pauline. "The streets are full of autos and trams and all sorts of vehicles". ...

"Ah, my dear child, it is awful not to see clearly. All those years that I've not been able to draw or paint, but had to be content with sculpture... And if my eyes keep getting worse, I won't even be able to sculpt. Then how will I pass the time?

I will surely die of boredom and disgust!... Dear Lord, what have I done that you punish me like this? My whole life has been devoted to my work; I have never sought honor or wealth... Dear God, please don't burden me now with blindness!" There was so much pain in his words that the young girl was moved, even though she had heard these complaints before. She tried to console him.

"Oh, no, monsieur Degas, you won't become blind, you mustn't believe it. Your eyes are just tired, because of the cold. As soon as the good weather returns, you'll feel better, I'm sure".

"Do you think so, Pauline?"

"I'm sure of it, monsieur Degas. And you'll see, your doctor will say the same thing. He'll tell you again how healthy you are for your seventy-six years. Think about it. You work every morning without rest, even Sundays and holidays. Plenty of younger artists don't do as much... And you eat well and your digestion is good, you sleep well, and you don't have rheumatism like your old friend, M. Rouart".

"But, Pauline, you forget my bladder problems".

"Well, that's what comes of being foolish when you were a young man," teased the model.

"Ah, you little minx, reminding me of my indiscretions..."

Edgar Degas: Female Nude Lying on Her Back. *c. 1865. Black chalk (10-7/16 x 13-13/16 in.). Cabinet des Dessins, The Louvre, Paris.*

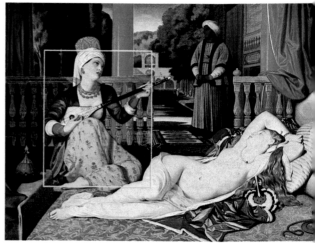

Jean-Auguste-Dominique Ingres (1780-1867): Study for Odalisque.
Black pencil (9-1/4 x 8 in.). Musée Ingres, Montauban.

Jean-Auguste-Dominique Ingres: Odalisque with Slave. *1842. Canvas.*
Walters Art Gallery, Baltimore.

Study for the Odalisque and *Odalisque with Slave* by Ingres

The preparatory study of the figure is important for the final composition of your work. The examples I have chosen for you show the preparatory study of a female figure alongside the finished painting, by Jean-Auguste-Dominique Ingres, the artist who so fascinated the young Degas when he was still a law student.

Degas took Ingres as his ideal and followed his example in order to achieve what he wanted in his own work.

He practiced diligently and was exasperatingly self-critical. He left nothing to chance, weighing and calculating everything, so that like the rhythms of music, a misplaced detail sounded as false as a wrong note in a musical score.

This is why for every motif that Degas drew, he corrected his work again and again, until he felt satisfied with its harmony and balance.

Unfortunately, this method of work is not followed much these days, especially by those artists who are busy trying to produce a certain quota of paintings each month in order to meet the demands of the market and their own pocketbooks; too often they end up focusing on quantity rather than quality.

Let's turn back to Jean-Auguste-Dominique Ingres and look at his drawing.

You will notice immediately that he changed the pose of his model, yet he left the original lines on the paper.

Compare the figure in the drawing to the one in the painting, and note the position Ingres finally chose for the slave.

Try to imagine the slave in the painting in the same position as the seated figure in the drawing, and you will see how the composition and balance of the painting would change.

The drawing of the slave was done with a soft pencil. The second tracing, made after his model changed position, was shaded more strongly to make the new pose stand out from the first. The superimposition of these two drawings creates a curious effect, similar to that obtained by film many years later.

A modified study, rethought and corrected, allowed the painter to study his subjects better and to arrange them in the most expressive way.

Studying the Figure: Drawings by the Great Masters

An analytical study of the figure offers a range of expressive possibilities. Observe the first example of *Nude Figure with Proportions Indicated*, by Michelangelo.

The human body is measured in relation to the head, and the head in relation to the nose. The distance that separates the chin from the hairline is the length of one hand. All the painters followed these mathematical rules rigorously. You can study them here as they are applied in the examples, and then you can draw up chart after chart of your own studies of proportions, volumes and perspectives.

Harmony was such an important calculation that it inspired Dürer to elaborate rules that could be handed down to posterity. At the end of the Renaissance, Michelangelo moved away from the idealized figure and invented a twisting or elongation of the body. This was an emotional reaction to these mathematical rules; later it was developed further by the Mannerists and then the Baroque artists. For them, the effects of the movement of muscles and expression prevailed over the rules of harmony.

When you do your studies, you may find a wooden mannequin will help you, especially with volume.

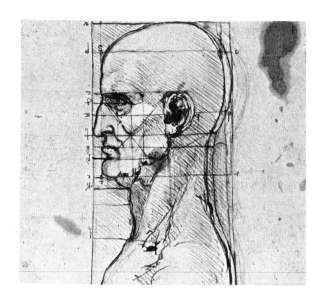

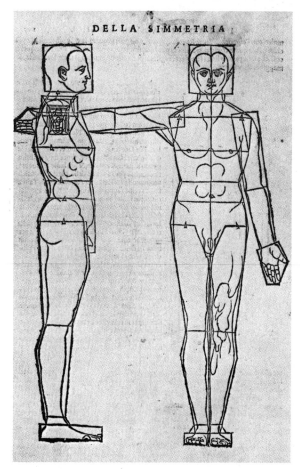

Above: Leonardo da Vinci: Proportions of the Human Face. *Pen and ink, watercolor highlights (13-1/2 x 9-5/8 in.). Accademia, Venice.*

Left: Michelangelo: Nude Figure with Proportions Indicated, *1516. Red pencil (11-3/8 x 7-1/16 in.). Royal Library, Windsor.*

Right: Albrecht Dürer: On the Symmetry of the Human Body, Book IV, *Venice 1591. Plate from book IV.*

Luca Cambiaso's *Study of Volumes* reproduced here, provides an example of the way to study volumes. His composition, defined as "cubist", is idealized and should be taken as a study of spatial forms.

Left: Luca Cambiaso (1527-85): Studies of Volumes. *Pen and bistre (13-3/8 x 9-7/16 in.). Gabinetto dei Disegni e delle Stampe, Uffizi, Florence.*

Right: Hans Holbein the Younger (1497-1593): Studies of Heads and Hands. *Pen and black ink (5 x 7-1/2 in.). Kupferstichkabinett, Kunstmuseum, Basel.*

117

The Portrait

Portraits tend to fall into one of two categories: those that focus on an interpretation of the lines of the face, with an attempt at characterization; and those that go beyond the individual characteristics to transform the sitter into an ideal. Of course, the concept of resemblance lies at the heart of portraiture.

Resemblance means those characteristics such as form, expression, look, posture, etc. which let us recognize the person portrayed.

Profile of a Young Man by **Andrea del Sarto**

Andrea del Sarto was one of the most interesting personalities in Florence at the beginning of the 16th century. Born in 1486, he began work as a goldsmith, then studied for a period with a minor painter before finally joining the workship of Piero di Cosimo, according to Vasari in *Lives of the Artists*.

He soon left Piero to open his own studio with Franciabigio, but his masters were Leonardo and Michelangelo.

Andrea del Sarto (1486-1531): Profile of a Young Man. *Red pencil (7-11/16 x 6-1/8 in.). Cabinet des Dessins, The Louvre, Paris.*

Like all the other painters of that era, he was fascinated by them, and, given their greatness, it was no mistake. Let's look now at the drawing Del Sarto did called *Profile of a Young Man*.

You can quickly see just how familiar the artist was with anatomy by looking at the contours and the facial muscles of the drawing.

You can also see how the hatching follows the movement of the muscles and models the face. But the most impressive element of the drawing is the effect produced by having the lighting coming from behind and focusing on the shoulders, neck, back of the head and part of the ears. The hair is barely defined in the areas in shadow, while in the highlighted areas it is not defined at all.

Drawing Hair

When learning to draw hair, it is important to suggest its volume through light and shadow, defining the limits of the areas of light and shade with small short strokes. Never draw hair strand by strand, or it will look like iron filings. Leave that to the "naif" painters.

If you look with half-closed eyes, you will see that even raven black hair has zones of light and shadow, and that the highlighted areas sometimes look white.

The same rule applies when drawing beards and moustaches.

Use your new skill at hatching to suggest hair. Copying models with thick long hair, like those in the drawings reproduced on the next page, is a very useful exercise. The drawings are two portraits of my daughter, done in 1980, that I think are particularly well suited to illustrate what I have been trying to explain.

Hair should be seen and conceived as a volume, so take care to preserve the zones of shade and light above all, using a few very dark strokes here and there where the hair forms dark fissures.

In a portrait, hair should be depicted with great care, for it is a very important feature, giving expression to the face.

Sometimes it is not even necessary to draw in the eyes, for the shadow over them builds the expression, as you can see in the example on the next page, done in red pencil.

You will often find such a solution used by the great masters. Every time you go to an exhibition, observe the portraits carefully and get into the habit of discovering the solutions that painters invented to achieve the effects they wanted. Fair hair needs only to be hinted at with some effective parallel strokes, in the shadow zones.

Drawing the Face

As you apply the rules I have given you, and begin to study more deeply — documenting what you learn so that nothing is left to chance — seek out sketches by the great masters and copy them in your notebook. Remember that Manet and Degas met at the Louvre, where they would go to copy the works on view (for the purpose of studying them, of course, not to make forgeries). Begin a drawing of the face by tracing the irregular geometric shape it forms, continuing, little by little, to build each detail. Do not begin by drawing one detail after the other, for you will lose sight of the whole and end up with portraits where one eye is lower than the other, and the nose is out of line. An error in portraying the eyes can make a person seem cross-eyed. Every point in the face should be aligned horizontally and vertically with another point. Looking for the cross points by placing a piece of tracing paper over a reproduction of a painting and following them is a good way to learn this.

The Eyes

Remember that the gaze is mobile, and the eyes are constantly changing expression and position: they can be wide open, half closed, barely open, looking up, looking down, etc. The eyelid plays

its part by varying the shape of the eye, as you can see in the details above.

Practice drawing this detail of the face by copying the eyes of your friends and figuring out their shadows. Keep in mind that the eye is round and covered by the eyelid, which makes a shadow over the area of the eye that it covers.

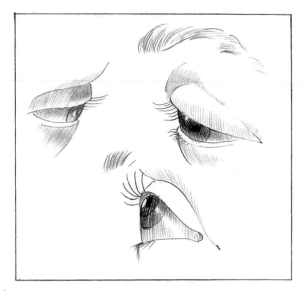

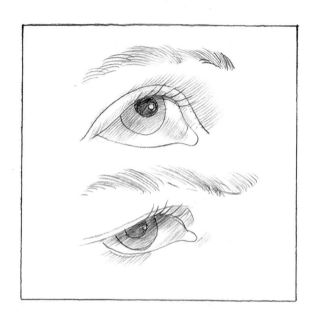

The Ears

Young painters often neglect this part of the head, but it is just as important as any other feature, and can add a great deal of character to the final portrait. Learn to sketch the overall shape of the ear first, then fill in the details. Keep in mind as you work that the outline will lead you to the details; eventually you will be able to draw from memory without always having to depend on a model.

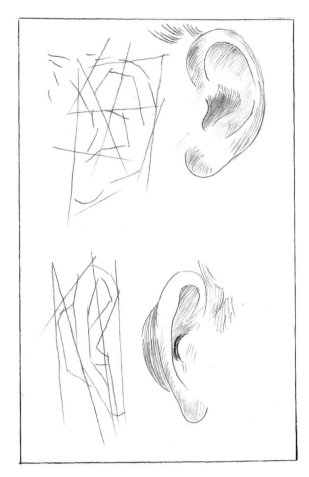

The Nose

The important thing to remember when drawing the nose is that it is the unit of measure when drawing the face. Most faces are divided into three parts, based on the length of the nose: from the hairline to the top of the nose; the length of the nose itself; and last, from the end of the nose to the chin (refer back to Leonardo's drawing on page 115).

At first, practice drawing this detail of the face by copying the works of the great masters. Look for a typical shape, such as an aquiline nose, and

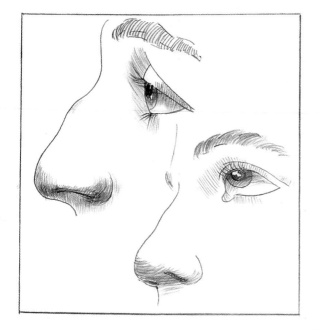

draw it from different angles: from above, from below, in three-quarters profile, etc. Practice drawing as many different noses as you can — do not let yourself become complacent in your work. Above all, remember to build your drawings. It is a slow method, but it will produce sat- isfying results, and, ultimately, it will give you the skill to tackle anything without fear.

The Mouth
Like the eyes, the mouth is an essential element in the expression of a face.

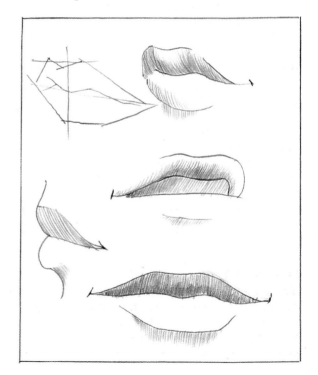

Try using your own mouth as a model, with the help of a mirror. Or, copy the drawings of the masters, especially those of the past who have produced drawings that cannot be easily duplicated without a certain understanding and constant practice. To reach such a level you must draw every chance you get, filling sheet after sheet. I can think of no other way.

Look at the mouths you see around you. No two are alike. They can be wide or narrow, fleshy or thin, childlike or sensual, depending on the line of the lips. Under normal light, the upper lip is always more in shadow than the lower, unless the light is coming from below. Then, of course, the situation is reversed.

Get into the habit of sketching a single detail over and over on the same sheet of paper, drawing it from different angles: straight on, in profile, etc. This will help you to memorize shapes. Each drawing you make will stick in your memory, and you will be able to go back and redo it when you want.

Drawing A Plaster-cast Skull

The group of skulls shown here were drawn by one of my students, Gianfranco Pugni, who, after a year of course work, became a good draftsman. He did this series of skulls while he was studying rotation. Before he could achieve this

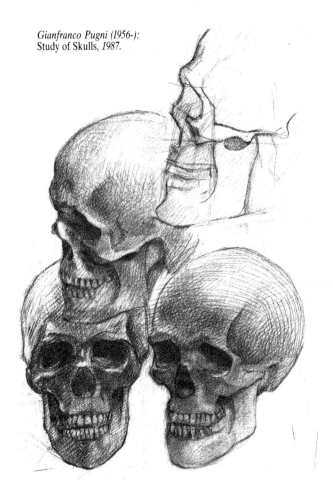

Gianfranco Pugni (1956-): Study of Skulls, 1987.

result, he made study after study to develop the skill necessary to draw the head, from memory, from any angle. To do this exercise yourself, you will, of course, need a skull. As it is not an easy object to find, it is better to buy a plaster cast of one in a specialty store or an art supplies store that is connected to an art school. The exercise should be done with the help of a plumb line, made according to my earlier instructions.

Draw the skull in the upper right hand corner of your paper, sketching the broad overall shape first, and then refining it as you figure out the measurements and the points that coincide. This is rather like fitting a shoe or a corset. When you put it on it is quite loose; as you tighten it, it molds to your shape.

When you have finished your outline, go on to the shading, using the hatching techniques most suitable for this drawing. With a 3B pencil, begin by lightly shading the parts in shadow with a soft gray tone, then continue on to the half-tones. Go back over the darkest zones, the areas in the light, and the half-tones, and then go back again to the darkest zones.

To work on the details, replace your 3B pencil with a harder 2B, and gradually accentuate the deepest shadows. To get in all the small details, work with a 1B pencil that will let you to do the fine work with the point. Define the shadows around the teeth, and try to construct the details within the areas of deep shadow. Lay down and blend your hatching so it gives a three-dimensional effect to your drawing. The only thing left to do after that is to create the highlights with a very clean eraser or, if you prefer, with a few strokes of a white pencil.

The Self-portrait

For an artist, the self-portrait can mean many different things. For one thing, it is the first time that, upon showing the results, you are not immediately accused by the person who has posed of making him look ugly and nothing at all like he is in real life. The self-portrait becomes a kind of training ground before the actual test. And as you draw your own face, you begin to realize that you can communicate to others the state of your soul.

For example, van Gogh attempted to portray in his self-portraits and portraits something that other artists did not see. Look at his two self-portraits on page 130. They will help you understand that great painters are confronted with the same problems that you will have. The first series of notes is made more interesting because of the details it shows: the nose drawn full face, and the lone left eye. The technique is one that we discussed when we were doing still-life drawings — pronounced lines that are full of feeling and searching for expression. The research of details that van Gogh carried out in his study reflects another quest going on inside him, one that was much more dramatic and striking: that of becoming a painter. For van Gogh, art became the "means for living", and the revealing letters to his brother Theo are a most sincere and passionate testimony to this belief.

I would like you to read a beautiful letter Vincent wrote to his brother at the time Vincent was attending drawing classes in Anvers. After reading it you will have an idea of what the painter was searching for in his class and what awaited him.

"Dear Theo,

I must tell you that I would be quite reassured if you could approve my project of coming to Paris much earlier than June or July. The more I think about it, the more desirable it seems.

Just think that if everything goes well, if I have good food and so on for that whole time — though I would probably not have everything I needed — even in that case, it would be six months before I could be completely recovered.

It would certainly take a lot more time if from March to July I had to undergo in Brabant everything that I have gone through here these last few months, and it probably would not make a great deal of difference.

At the moment I feel quite weak, worse even, because of the work I must do, but that is the normal course of events, nothing extraordinary. But it is a matter of getting my strength back. In Brabant I will again be spending my last cent on models, and so it will be the same old story and I don't think that is good. We will stray from our course that way. I beg you then to let me come sooner, even right away.

I would rent a garret in Paris and take my paint box and drawing material, then I could finish the most urgent things, those studies from the ancients, which will certainly be of great help to me when I go to Cormon. I can go to the Louvre or the Ecole des Beaux-Arts to draw.

As for the other things, before getting started in a new place, we can do some projects and get everything better organized. If I must, I will go to Nuenen for the month of March to see how things are going, and how everyone is and see if I can find some models there. If not, and I imagine that will be the case, I could go to Paris at the end of March and begin to draw at the Louvre for example.

I have thought a great deal about what you wrote concerning renting a studio but I think it would be good to look for one together and before we

Vincent van Gogh: Self Portraits, *1888.*

decide to live together definitively we should live near each other. I suggest starting by renting a garret, from April to June, for example.

Then I would feel at home again in Paris when I go to Cormon's. That way I would also be in better spirits.

I must tell you that, even though I continue to attend, the pedantry of those fellows at the Academy is often quite unbearable and they seem quite hateful to me at times. But I try very hard to avoid arguments with them and go my own way. I feel like I am getting closer to what I am looking for and perhaps I will find it sooner if I can do what I want to do when I draw those plaster reproductions.

Altogether I am happy to have gone to the Academy, because I have had many opportunities to see the results of "prendre par le contour".

They practice this systematically and they are always trying to pick a quarrel with me over it. "Faites d'abord un contour, votre contour n'est pas juste, je ne corrigerai pas ça, si vous modelez avant d'avoir sérieusement arrêté votre contour". ("First, draw an outline. You haven't got the outline right. I refuse to correct it if you are going to model it before you have finished your outline"). You can see how it always ends up at the same point. You can't imagine how flat, insipid and lifeless the results of this system are; I must say

that I am content to have seen the thing up close. Like David, or even worse, like a Pieneman in full regalia. I have wanted to say twenty-five times, "Your outline is a trick". But it doesn't seem worth fighting about. And yet even when I keep silent, they irritate me and I irritate them. But this is not very important. The point is to get to know the process extremely well. So consequently, patience and perserverance.

They always say, "Color and models are not important, you can learn about them very quickly; what is the most essential and the most difficult is the outline".

As you see, one learns new things at the Academy. I didn't realize color and models were so easy.

Yesterday I finished the drawing I made for the competition of the evening class. It is the figure of Germanicus which you know. I know for certain that I will come in last because the others' drawings all resemble each other and mine is completely different. I saw the one that is supposed to be the best while it was being drawn; I was sitting right behind the man who drew it. It is done correctly and is everything you might want, but it is dead and so are all the other drawings I have seen.

Enough. Let these worries torment us so that they fire us up to pursue something more noble.

And I will force myself to wait.

You too need a life that is more intense. If we do get together, together we will know more than we each know separately; this way we will be able to do more.

By the way, have you noted Paul Mantz's subtle remark: "In life, women are perhaps the supreme difficulty", that phrase that is in his article on Baudry.

We will find that out, at least if we have not already done so.

I read with interest a chapter in Zola's *Works* on Gil Blas. There is a remarkable description of an argument between the painter — probably Manet — and a woman who posed for him and had quickly grown indifferent towards him. What one learns at the Academy is that it is better not to paint women. One only rarely has a woman posing nude — never in class and only rarely in private.

Even in the classes where we draw from antique models, there are ten figures of men for every female figure. It is very comfortable...

Of course in Paris the situation will be better and in fact it seems to me that one learns a lot by constantly comparing the male figure to the female for they are different in so many ways. Women may be the "supreme difficulty" but what would life and art be without them?

Good-bye, write to me soon.

Vincent"

P.S. If I go to Nuenen in March it will be to help with the moving, but I should go anyway to change residence. Personally, I would be quite happy not to return".

After that long parenthesis about van Gogh, the painter of self-portraits full of tension and incomparable expressiveness, let's go back to the main subject of this chapter, namely what a self-portrait is about. Sometimes such a painting is born during a period when an artist is passing through a crisis, and it serves as a safety valve for the existential angst that may suddenly well up for no apparent reason. At other times, listening to music or to someone reading a poem can conjure up images with which to identify.

Such a case can be seen in a series of self-portraits that I drew after I read a poem written by a friend of mine, someone who I think is a very fine poet, although he is not well known. His name is Antonio Agriesti. The poem he wrote is called *Vortex* and as you can see, the lay-out of the type suggests the image evoked by the title, a little like Apollinaire's *Calligrammes*.

I hope you will read his lines thoughtfully and that you will take inspiration from them, too,

Vortex
Like a river
You sweep everything away
          Including yourself
And meanwhile one by one you watch
          The vortexes
                    which you make which make you
                              the vortex that you write
                                        on the surface of the water
                                                  first runes of the world
                                                            first and last hieroglyphics of all
                                                                      that are reduced vortex by vortex
                                                                                to nothing.

Vortex by vortex
So much water goes by
You became earth air
          fire and flames
          And then again
                    Vortex by vortex
                              Belly by belly
                                        Reed/tree/man/daemon
                                        and demon
                                        Love knot, death knot
                                        White dove in flight
                                        against the crow-like blackness
                                                  of Night.
                                                            Antonio Agriesti

and be moved to do a self-portrait. When you do, look at yourself in the mirror, at first full-face, then in profile; work with the mirror as if it were a real subject.

Do this exercise with a soft pencil (3B or 4B);

alternatively, you might try a sanguine or sepia pencil. Construct your drawing carefully and methodically on your easel. Draw in the details with precision, following the suggestions and advice I have given you.

More Self-portraits: Degas and Cézanne

The portraits painted by the young Degas around 1855 show us a melancholic and reserved man. We get a similar impression from the portraits he did of his brothers and sisters during the same period: they express the sadness of youth weighed down by a strict upbringing and the lack of a mother's love (their mother died when Degas was 13).

As you look at the self-portrait of Degas reproduced here, observe how the lines in the face denote a natural seriousness of expression: the elongated face, the haggard eyes under high arched brows, well-defined lips, and a slightly rounded forehead. All the lines in the face are drawn down to the last detail, with light hatching suggesting the beard, and the hair and sideburns perfectly detailed. The only part of the drawing that leaps out at you is the dark band of the tie. This was achieved by doing layers of cross-hatching in ink, in contrast to the delicate tones of the face, and it reinforces the sad, serious expression. In Degas's portraits of the period, the psychological study predominates, following the tradition of the French painter Clouet. When doing a self-portrait, Degas searched his own face for

Edgar Degas: Self Portrait, *1856. Pencil and brown ink (9-3/4 x 7 in.). Cabinet des Dessins, The Louvre, Paris.*

the answers to his identity.

Compare this to the self-portrait Cézanne did around 1880 when he was forty-one (he was born in 1839).

At first glance, one has the impression that the artist sketched the portrait hastily, almost as if from memory. Oddly enough, Cézanne does not reveal anything in this portrait of himself, neither his feelings, his passions nor his thoughts. This is true of his self-portraits in general. Yet, they are very revealing, in the sense that the painter clings to his independence to such an extent that he seems to express defiance, a look that says, "I will not be trapped", thereby escaping any influence that might contaminate or stain the "purity" of his art.

Paul Cézanne: Self Portrait, *around 1880. Pencil on greyish-brown cartridge paper (12x8 in.). Kupferstichkabinett, Kunstmuseum, Basel.*

136

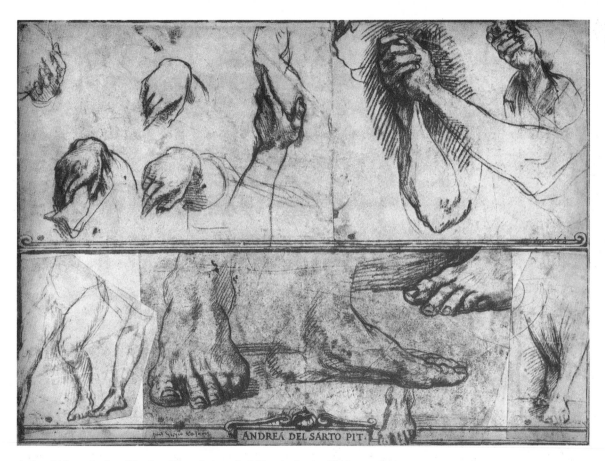

Andrea del Sarto: Studies of Hands and Feet. *Red pencil. Cabinet des Dessins, The Louvre, Paris.*

Andrea del Sarto: Studies of Hands. *Red pencil. Gabinetto dei Disegni e delle Stampe, Uffizi, Florence.*

Studies of Hands and Feet by Andrea del Sarto

We must not overlook the upper and lower extremities of the body. It is important to avoid the imperfections that I see in the works of many modern figurative artists, who devote most of their efforts to interpretation in order to hide their other weaknesses.

Observe the drawings by Andrea del Sarto on pages 137 and 138, which are elegant examples of the study of details carried out by the Renaissance artists, the kind of work that students were frequently given to copy.

Let me repeat once more how important it is to copy the works of the great masters. It is a very useful exercise, one that will give you the confidence to tackle drawings directly from nature. Copying from photographs, on the other hand, is of very little value.

After you have done many drawings from nature, it is important to try to draw fragments of the human figure from memory.

Studies of Hands on Brown Wrapping Paper

Look at the pleasant effect produced by drawing with sanguine or pencil on the pale brown background of wrapping paper. The lines of the soft pencil are warm, thick, and full of emotion. To do this exercise, begin by sketching the hand,

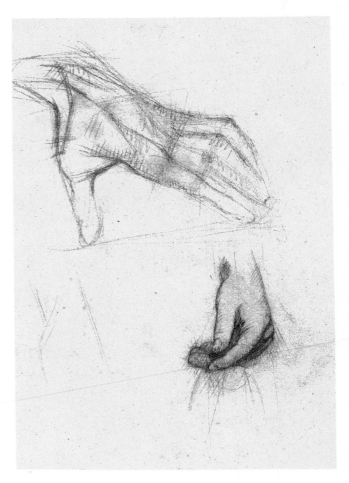

139

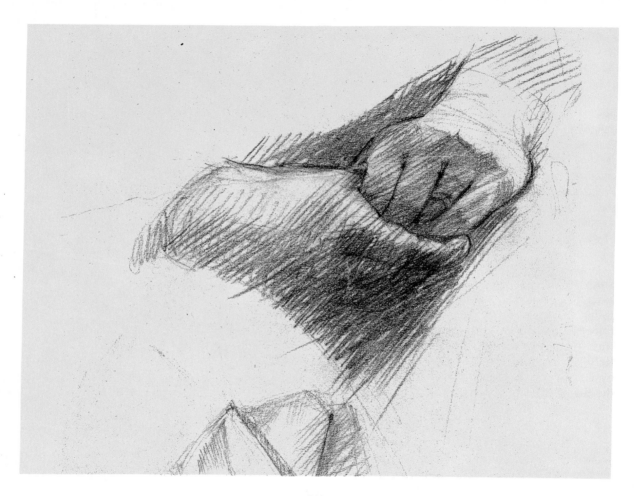

shaping first the muscles underneath the skin, then constructing it according to the usual methods, which you can see in the study of the open hand on the previous page. Define the shadows, taking care not to neglect those in the background the ones cast on the surface upon which the hands are resting.

Do not underestimate the importance of the shading that models the muscles, for that is what gives volume to the drawing.

Practice constructing hands in all sorts of natural poses before you go on to the next study, that of the clothed figure in poses taken from moments of everyday life.

Study for Dressing by Mary Cassatt

Mary Cassatt was an extraordinary Impressionist painter. Born in Pittsburgh in 1845, she sailed to Europe at the age of twenty and, with the goal of studying the old masters, she travelled to France, Italy, Spain and Holland. In 1877 she was invited by Degas, who had seen some of her works at the Salon of 1874 in Paris, to become part of a

Mary Cassatt (1845-1926): Study for Dressing, 1891. Black pastel and pencil (15-1/2 x 10-7/8 in.). Rosenwald Collection, National Gallery, Washington, D.C.

group of Impressionists, and to participate in their exhibitions. She learned from Degas (who was a strong influence on her), Zandomeneghi and Manet to "see the figure" in poses from everyday life.

The drawing on the preceding page is an example of this. If you look at it at length, you almost feel as if you are part of the scene, that you are there in the room next to the seated woman arranging her hair. The reflection in the mirror accentuates the impression one has of participating directly in the scene. The linear solution is wonderful, a lesson Mary Cassatt learned from the drawings of Ingres, which she came to know through Degas.

The drawing was done with a combination of pencil and pastel crayon. She did the basic sketch with pencil, with no shading, then she accentuated the contours and dark mass of hair of both the actual figure and the figure in the mirror with a black pastel crayon, as if to focus the gaze of the viewer there on the simple activity that gives the drawing its name.

This technique has been used by other painters in their preliminary sketches for wood cuts.

At first glance, the drawing might seem to be a rapid sketch capturing one moment in a day: an impression, as it were. Yet, it has as much value as drawings with seemingly more refined shading. The artist has succeeded in this case in creating the effect of volume by using different intensities and tonalities of lines.

But be careful. Do not choose just any technique that comes along. Be selective, choosing those that are most suitable to the demands of the moment and to your own artistic sensibilities.

Study this drawing and evaluate the details. If you think you would like to copy it, first try to analyze where Mary Cassatt used her pencil with full pressure and where she worked with a light touch. Afterwards, you can recreate the scene with a live model.

Portrait of Madame d'Haussonville by Ingres

Ingres was a highly demanding academic artist, a veritable despot, in fact, and events happening around him did not affect him in the least. The polemic that he created, the ideas that he stood for, and above all, the fact that he represented tradition, produced a strong reaction against him and his kind, culminating in the birth of Impressionism.

The writer Charles Baudelaire was very critical of him and wrote:

"What are the drawings like by Monsieur Ingres? Of high quality? Very intelligent? Anyone who has compared the different styles of the great

Jean-Auguste-Dominique Ingres:
Portrait of Madame d'Haussonville,
1842-45. Lead pencil (9-1/4 x 11-5/8
in.). Fogg Art Museum, Harvard
University, Cambridge
(Massachusetts).

masters will understand me when I say that Monsieur Ingres's drawings are the drawings of a systematic man... Monsieur Ingres has not looked at nature, nature has desecrated the painter".

Baudelaire, on the other hand, highly praised another of his contemporaries, Eugène Delacroix, defining him as "passionately in love with passion", "triumphant in every genre", "an essentially personal genius".

For many, Ingres represented not just an artist but a school, someone either to follow or to react against, a master who constantly defied other painters such as Courbet, Delacroix, Manet, Millet and Corot, all of whom opposed him.

This no longer happens today. With some rare exceptions, art school students no longer find in their teachers models to imitate. Today the only thing that exists is individualism. Even teachers have lost some of their fire and do not pass on to their students the sacred flame of art and a desire to experience as much as possible so each student can find his or her own path.

Personally, I have always felt pushed on in my artistic endeavors by something coming from within, something that makes me want to learn as many different techniques as I can, so I can express what I feel through my paintings and drawings. I do this for myself, and not for money or for recognition. That is why I admire such charismatic figures as Ingres.

Look at the drawing on page 143 and notice that it has been sub-divided into squares, the way I explained to you early in the book. Look at how the figure is reflected in the mirror, as in Mary Cassatt's drawing. As you may notice, the drawing is just a sketch done with a lead pencil. Only the face is given more detail and is lightly shaded. Imagine if you went over the outlines with a 6B pencil or a black pastel crayon. You would end up with a drawing that was like one of Mary Cassatt's.

To close, novelty is the child of the past. Cézanne the innovator, for example, studied and interpreted the classics; the father of abstract art, Piet Mondrian, came from a figurative artistic background. No artist can ignore what went before him. It is only through study and a deep understanding of previous experience that one can create something new.

Study of a Seated Figure

I drew this picture about twelve years ago. My wife, who is also a painter and thus aware of what was required of her, posed for me.

This sketch was made with a 6B pencil on brown wrapping paper almost three feet long. The sketch, drawn with a light touch, extends lengthwise, an easier way to portray the whole figure. You should always begin with the head, so as not to risk drawing the figure out of proportion. Do not forget that the head is the unit of measure for the rest of the body, so, if you begin there, everything else should fall into place.

After sketching the outline, I went on to define the shadows and to fill in the half-tones and deep shading, beginning again with the head. If you look closely you will see that the hands are the same as the ones in the study of details I showed you earlier. When you do yours, have your model assume a pose as close to this one as possible, and begin with the general outline. Then go on to refine it and balance the proportions.

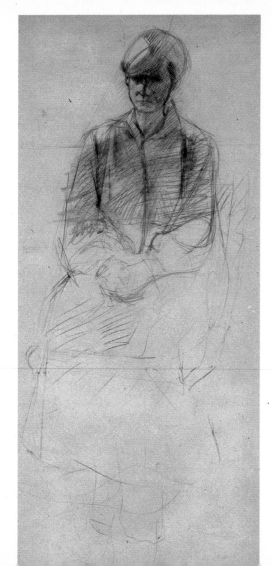

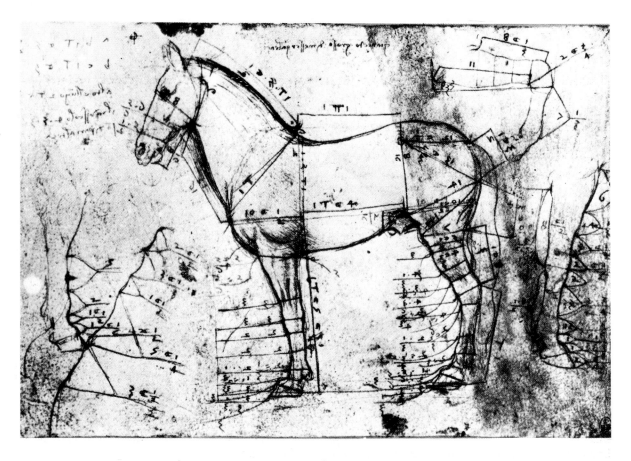

Leonardo da Vinci: The Proportions of the Horse. *Silverpoint on prepared blue paper. F.12319. Royal Library, Windsor.*

DRAWING ANIMALS

To learn to draw animals, you must follow the same rules that you learned when drawing people. This means beginning by studying plastercasts, statues, and especially equestrian monuments. You might find it helpful to visit a natural science museum, where you will be able to see either the skeleton or the animal itself. Then you can copy it from different angles, safe in the knowledge that it will not fidget or move about. And, as always, turn to the great masters and copy their drawings, especially those who were born before 1900, when the academic training of the time encouraged them to draw a cat to look like a cat, so you do not have to guess what it is. The animal that is most often portrayed in drawings is the horse. It has been captured moving about, standing still, in a pasture, in a stall, out on the battlefield and walking down a country lane.

Before trying to sketch a moving animal, however, you should let your work mature a bit. It is only with a thorough understanding of the structure of the animal that you will be able to draw it from memory.

Look at this study of a horse drawn by Leonardo. He, more than any other, was an artist who worked with every medium and portrayed all subjects. His investigations eventually enabled him to establish new rules of construction, based on a model that he himself discovered, which used the length of the horse's head as the unit of measure.

A Few Pages from Pierre Bonnard's Notebook
Pierre Bonnard drew constantly, covering his pocket diaries with sketches.

Look at the four sketches on the next page that come from his diary. They are done with confident, expressive strokes, and were most likely made with a 3B pencil.

Using the drawing on the page for December 3, 1934 as inspiration, the painter made a very fine oil painting two years later, called *Circus Horse*. In another notebook from 1931, we find some drawings of cats. Cats have been loved by many artists, myself included, partly because when they come into our houses, they make themselves comfortable on a cushion or an armchair or next to the heater and stay still long enough to be drawn.

These drawings from Bonnard's diary capture

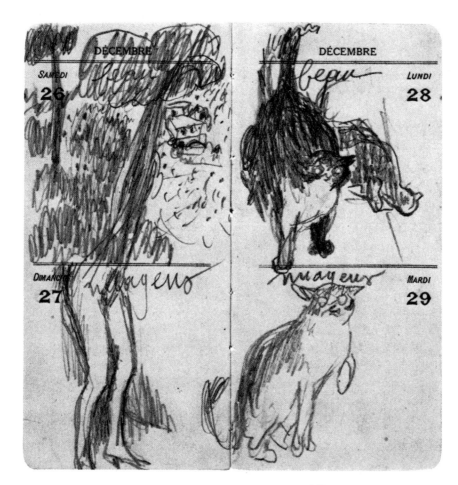

Pierre Bonnard: Page from his diary, *1931.*

them at two particular moments, when they are eating and when they are washing themselves after they have finished. In the drawing for December 28, the black and white cat in the foreground seems as if it has been interrupted during the meal, while the one in the background continues to eat. The cat in the square for the 29th, with one paw raised, looks as if it had already eaten and was cleaning itself when distracted by the artist.

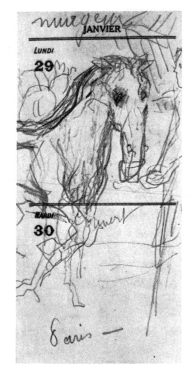

Pierre Bonnard: Page from his diary, *1934.*

The Horses of Eugène Delacroix

The horses that Delacroix drew or painted in his notebooks or on canvasses have one characteristic in common: they are always captured in movement. Whether rearing up in a clash between two soldiers or falling wounded during battle, they are always in epic poses.

The drawings you see here were done by Delacroix in Morocco in 1832. Let's read an extract from a letter he wrote to J.B. Pierret from Tangier, in which he describes a horse fight.

"Two of the horses got into a fight and I witnessed the most relentless battle you can imagine: all the furies that Gros and Rubens invented were as nothing compared to this. After being bitten all over as they climbed on top of each other, walking on their hind legs like men, having naturally thrown their riders, they threw themselves into a small river where the battle continued with unparalleled fury. It took the devil's strength to tear them apart".

Left: Eugène Delacroix (1798-1863): Moroccan Horseman Charging. *Lead pencil (6-15/16 x 5-1/16 in.). Cabinet des Dessins, The Louvre, Paris.*

Right: Eugène Delacroix: Detail of Moroccan Mounting a Horse. *Size of the whole drawing (9-3/4 x 15 in.). Cabinet des Dessins, The Louvre, Paris.*

Studies of Cats by Gainsborough and Géricault

In its personality, its movements and its postures, the cat gives us the chance to study a synthetic line (sinuous and continuous) that ex-

presses its character, as you can see in the studies below by Thomas Gainsborough (1727-1788). The rapid sketches of Théodore Géricault (1791-1824) on the opposite page, by their immediacy and unfinished nature, testify to being taken from life; they attempt to catch the movements, expressions and details of the head and legs.

Right: Thomas Gainsborough (1727-1788): Cat Studies, c. 1765. Charcoal, tempera and white chalk (12-11/16 x 18-1/16 in.). Rijksmuseum, Amsterdam.

2-2-2o

Young Girl With Cat by Gianni Maimeri

This quick sketch, dated February 2, 1920, shows the extraordinary spontaneity so typical of the work of this prolific Italian artist (1884-1951) who has been unfairly ignored by the critics and art dealers.

The scene he captured could not have lasted for more than a few moments, but it was long enough for Maimeri to fix it in his memory and then to duplicate it in his sketchbook with a lightning quickness that is typical of great artists.

My Cat

As I said, cats are animals of which I am very fond. I have drawn them many times and studied them thoroughly, endlessly portraying them in their most typical postures. From experience, I would advise you to practice drawing them at first when they are asleep as I did in my drawing, but you must be very quiet; if bothered they will wake up, making brusque movements, and unlike a human model, they will not go back to their previous pose. I suggest you do several

Gianni Maimeri (1884-1951): Young Girl with Cat, *1920. Private collection, Milan.*